Draw 50

BOATS, SHIPS,

TRUCKS & TRAINS

BOOKS IN THIS SERIES

Draw **50**

BOATS,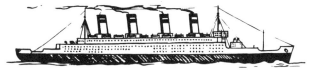

SHIPS,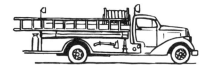

TRUCKS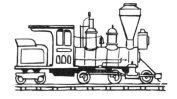

& TRAINS

Lee J. Ames

BROADWAY BOOKS
NEW YORK

BROADWAY

Published by Broadway Books
a division of Random House, Inc.
1540 Broadway, New York, New York 10036

BROADWAY BOOKS and it's logo, a letter B bisected on the diagonal, are
trademarks of Broadway Books, a division of Random House, Inc.

Library of Congress Catalog Card Number 75-19011

Library of Congress Cataloging-in-Publication Data

Ames, Lee J.
  Draw 50 boats, ships, trucks & trains.

  Summary: Step-by-step instructions for drawing a variety of boats,
ships, trucks, and trains.
    1. Ships in art—Juvenile literature.   2. Boats in art—Juvenile
literature.   3. Trucks in art—Juvenile literature.   4. Railroads in art—
Juvenile literature.   5. Drawing—Technique—Juvenile literature.
[1. Drawing—Technique]   I. Title
NC825.S5A43   1987   743'.89629046

ISBN: 0-385-08903-1 Trade
       0-385-23630-1 Paperback

Printed in the United States of America

30 29 28 27 26 25 24 23 22

To *Mom* and *Toby* and most especially to the memory of
Pop

To the Reader

This book will show you a way to draw boats, ships, trucks and trains. You need not start with the first illustration. Choose whichever you wish. When you have decided, follow the step-by-step method shown. *Very lightly* and *carefully,* sketch out step number one. However, this step, which is the easiest, should be done *most carefully.* Step number two is added right to step number one, also lightly and also very carefully. Step number three is sketched right on top of numbers one and two. Continue this way to the last step.

It may seem strange to ask you to be extra careful when you are drawing what seem to be the easiest first steps, but this is most important because a careless mistake at the beginning may spoil the whole picture at the end. As you sketch out each step, watch the spaces between the lines, as well as the lines, and see that they are the same. After each step, you may want to lighten your work by pressing it with a kneaded eraser (available at art supply stores).

When you have finished, you may want to redo the final step in India ink with a fine brush or pen. When the ink is dry, use the kneaded eraser to clean off the pencil lines. The eraser will not affect the India ink.

Here are some suggestions: In the first few steps, even when all seems quite correct, you might do well to hold your work up to a mirror. Sometimes the mirror shows that you've twisted the drawing off to one side without being aware of it. At first you may find it difficult to draw the boxes, triangles or circles, or to just make the pencil go

where you wish. Don't be discouraged. The more you prac-
tice, the more you will develop control. Use a compass or a
ruler if you wish; professional artists do! The only equip-
ment you'll need will be a medium or soft pencil, paper, the
kneaded eraser and, if you wish, a compass, ruler, pen or
brush.

The first steps in this book are shown darker than nec-
essary so that they can be clearly seen. (Keep your work
very light.)

Remember, there are many other ways and methods to
make drawings. This book shows just one method. Why
don't you seek out other ways and methods to make drawings—from teachers, from libraries and, most importantly
. . . from inside yourself?

LEE J. AMES

To the Parent or Teacher

"David can draw a speedboat better than anybody else!" Such peer acclaim and encouragement generate incentive. Contemporary methods of art instruction (freedom of expression, experimentation, self-evaluation of competence and growth) provide a vigorous, fresh-air approach for which we must all be grateful.

New ideas need not, however, totally exclude the old. One such is the "follow me, step-by-step" approach. In my young learning days this method was so common, and frequently so exclusive, that the student became nothing more than a pantographic extension of the teacher. In those days it was excessively overworked.

This does not mean that the young hand is never to be guided. Rather, specific guiding is fundamental. Step-by-step guiding that produces satisfactory results is valuable even when the means of accomplishment are not fully understood by the student.

The novice with a musical instrument is frequently taught to play simple melodies as quickly as possible, well before he learns the most elemental scratchings at the surface of music theory. The resultant self-satisfaction, pride in accomplishment, can be a significant means of providing motivation. And all from mimicking an instructor's "Do-as-I-do . . ."

Mimicry is prerequisite for developing creativity.

We learn the use of our tools by mimicry. Then we can use those tools for creativity. To this end I would offer the budding artist the opportunity to memorize or mimic (rotelike, if you wish) the making of "pictures." "Pictures" he has been anxious to be able to draw.

The use of this book should be available to anyone who *wants* to try another way of flapping his wings. Perhaps he will then get off the ground when his friend says, "David can draw a speedboat better than anybody else!"

LEE J. AMES

Draw 50

BOATS, SHIPS, TRUCKS & TRAINS

Cabin Cruiser

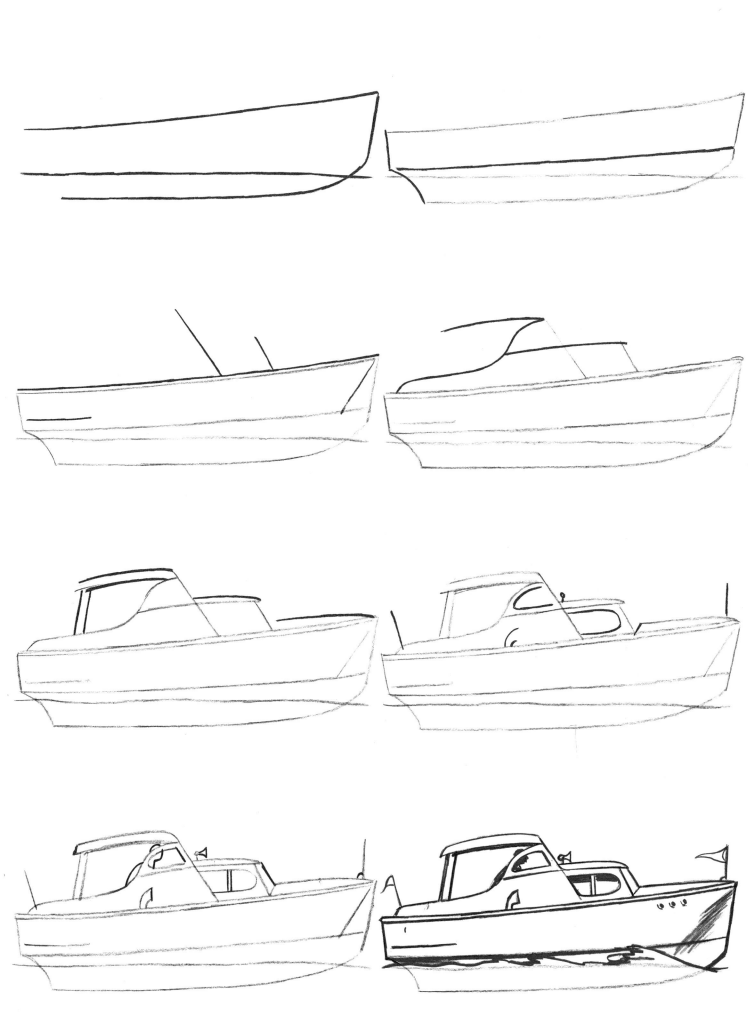

Paddle-wheel Houseboat

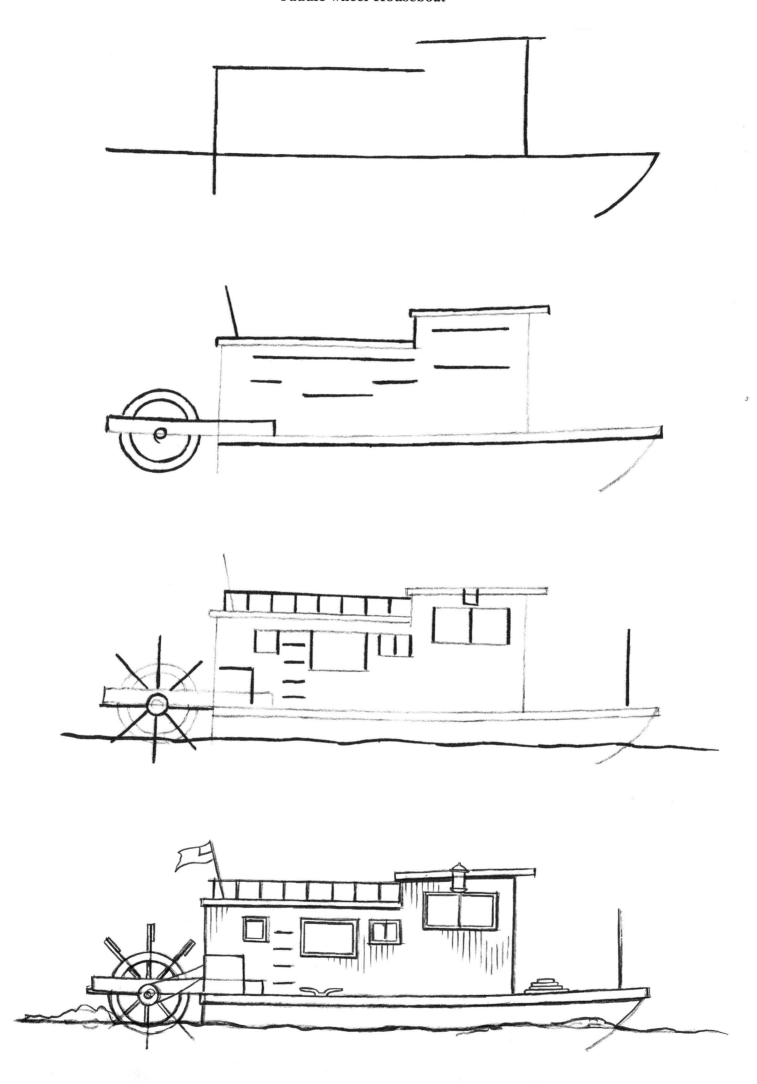

Racing Craft

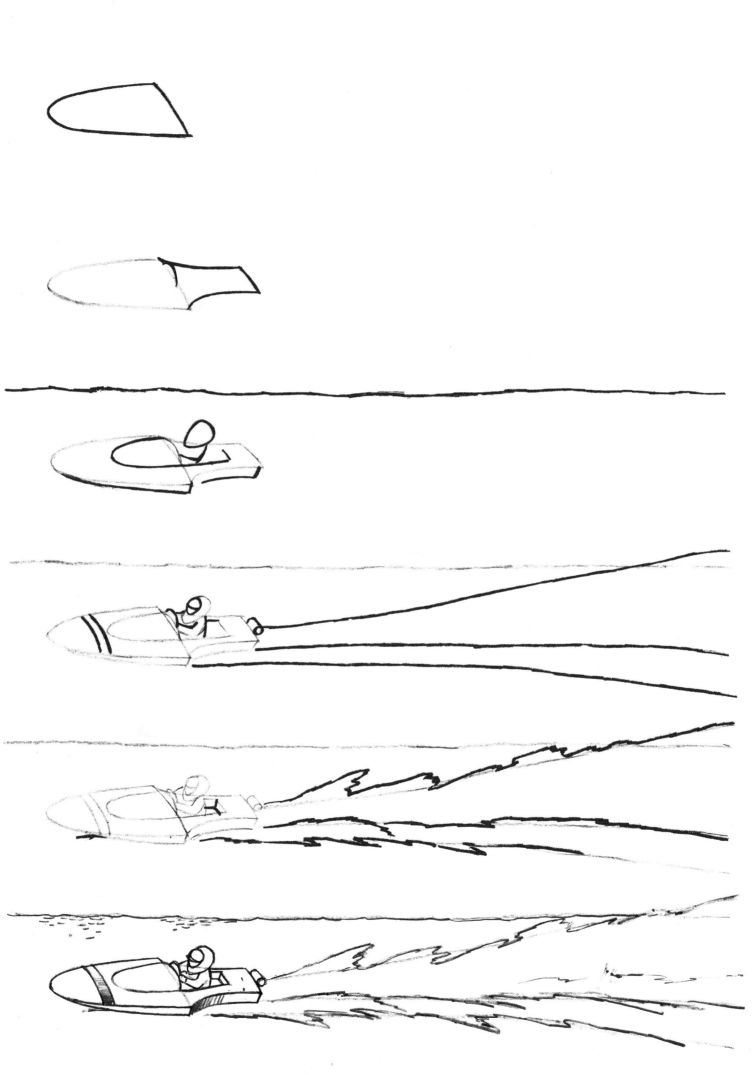

Outboard Speedboat

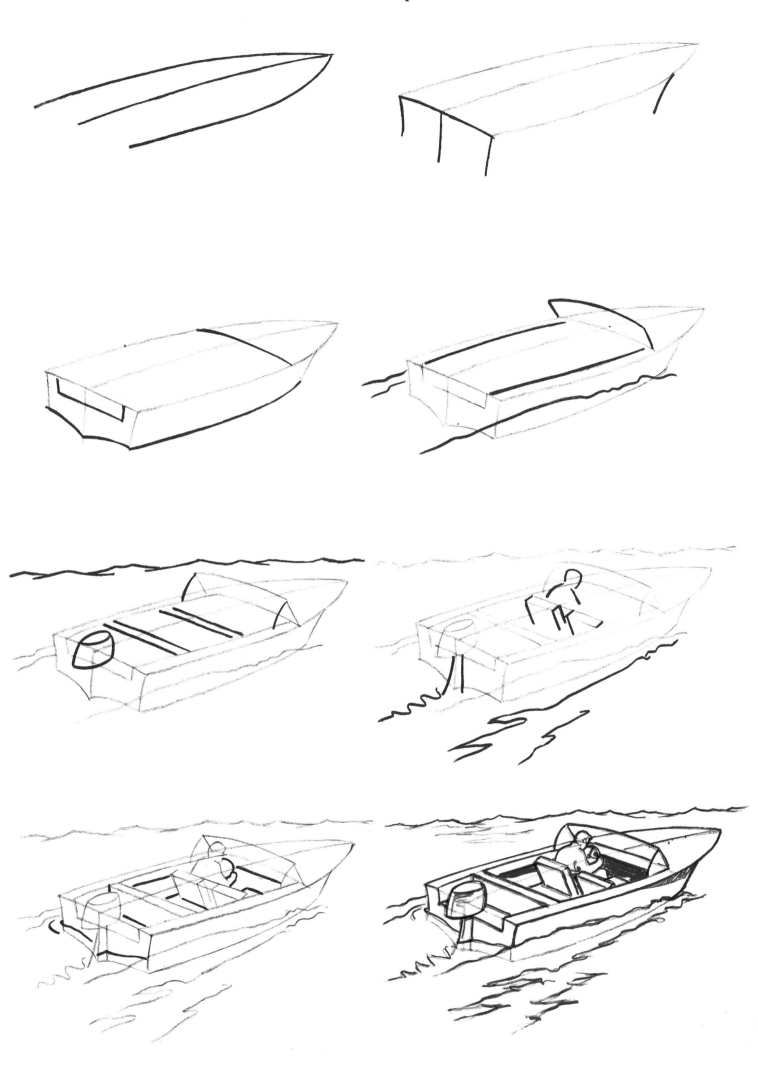

Mini-tugboat

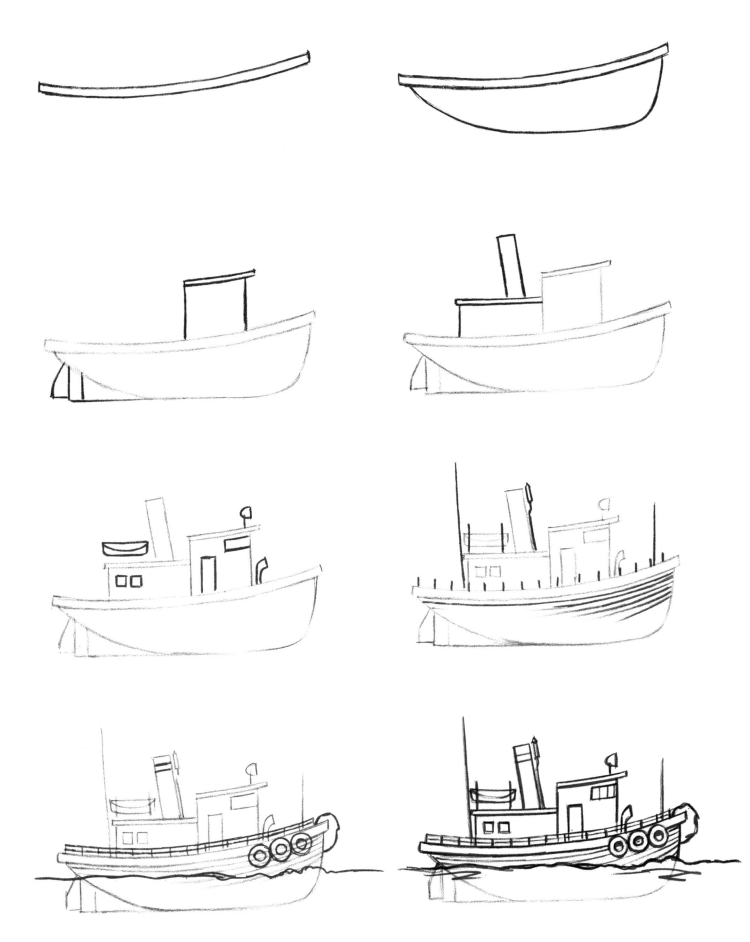

Fishing Boat (Liner)

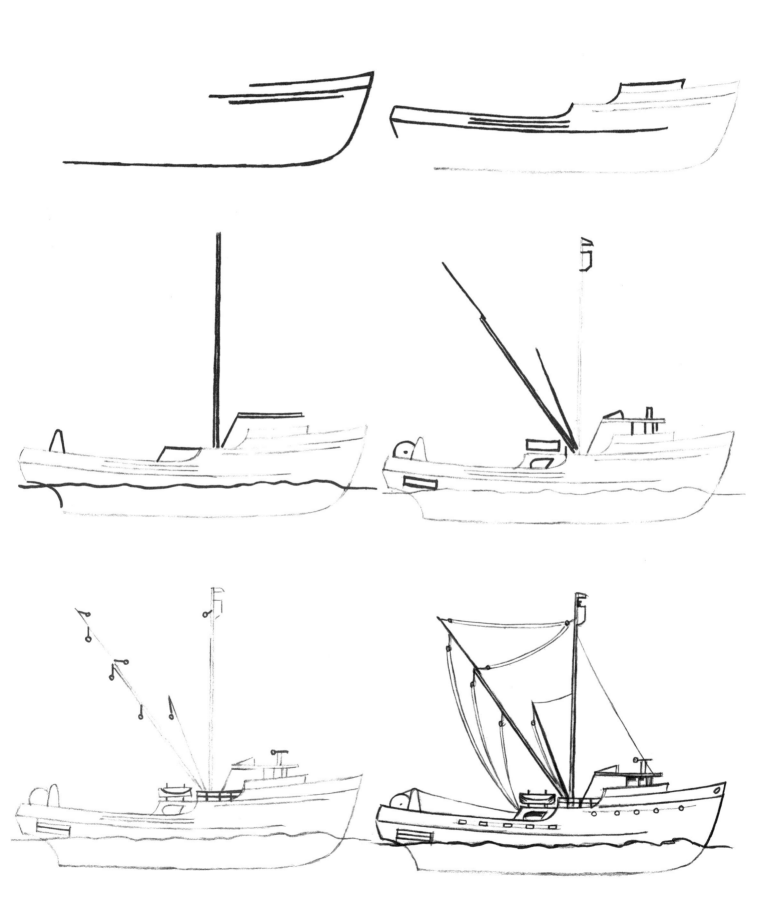

Yacht

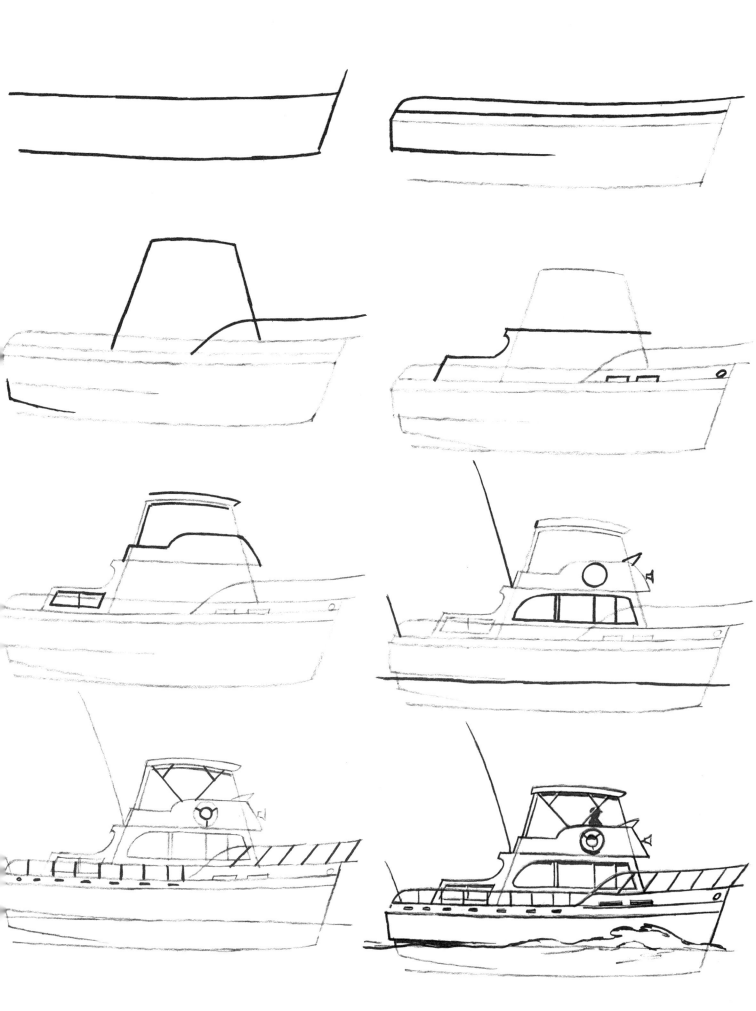

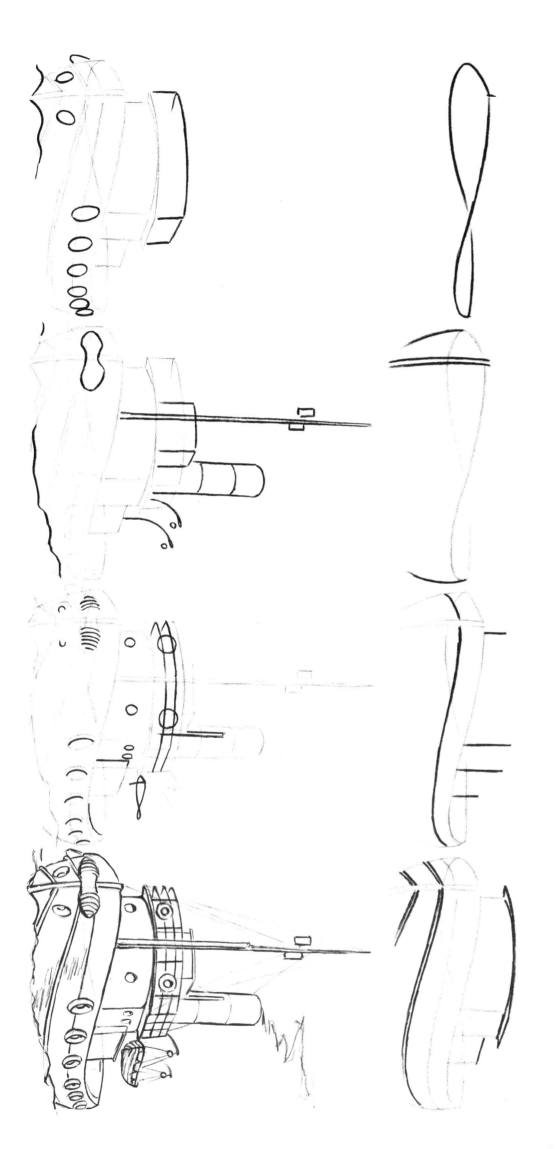

Tugboat

Tanker

Paddle-wheel Steamer

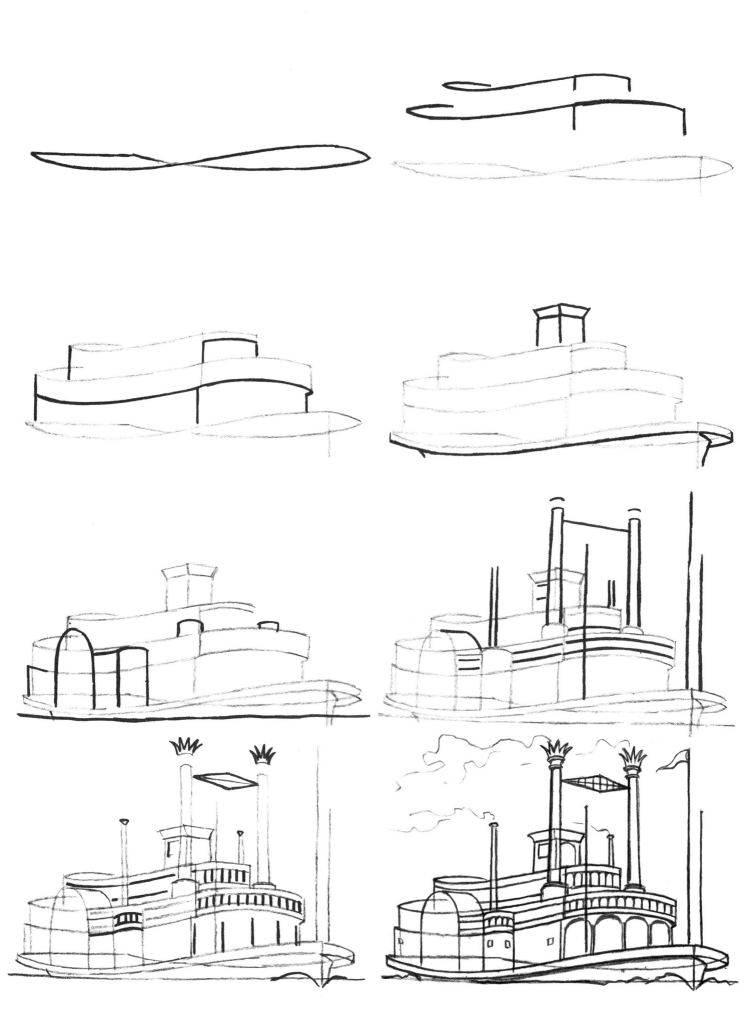

Ocean Liner

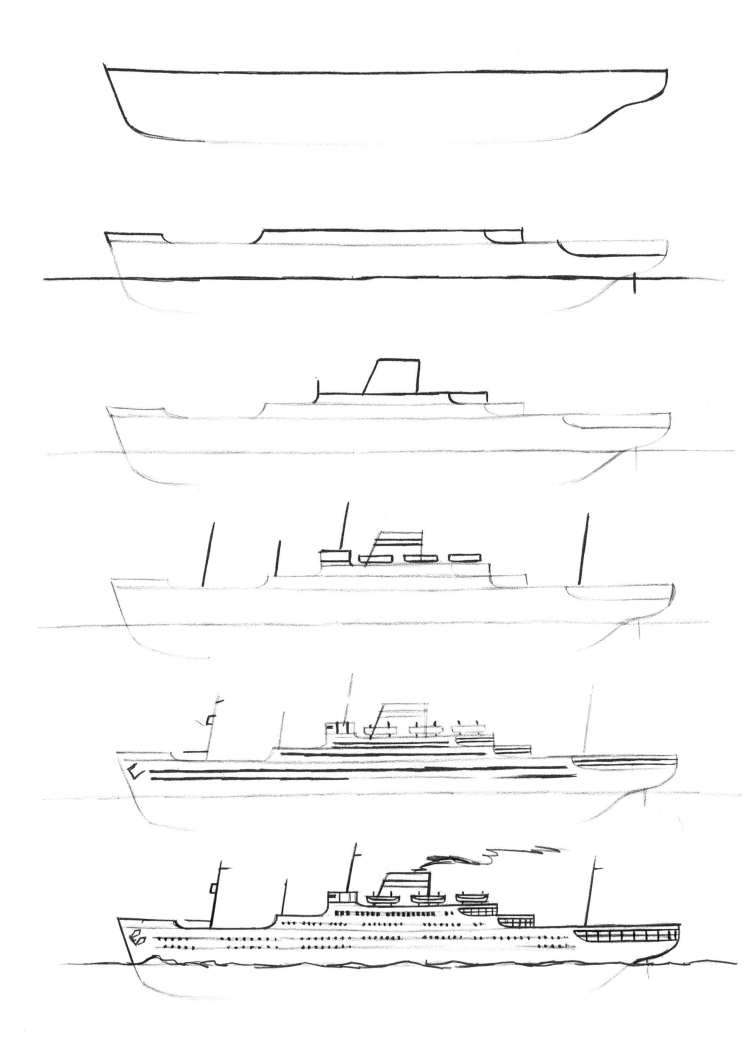

Ocean Liner (Early Twentieth Century)

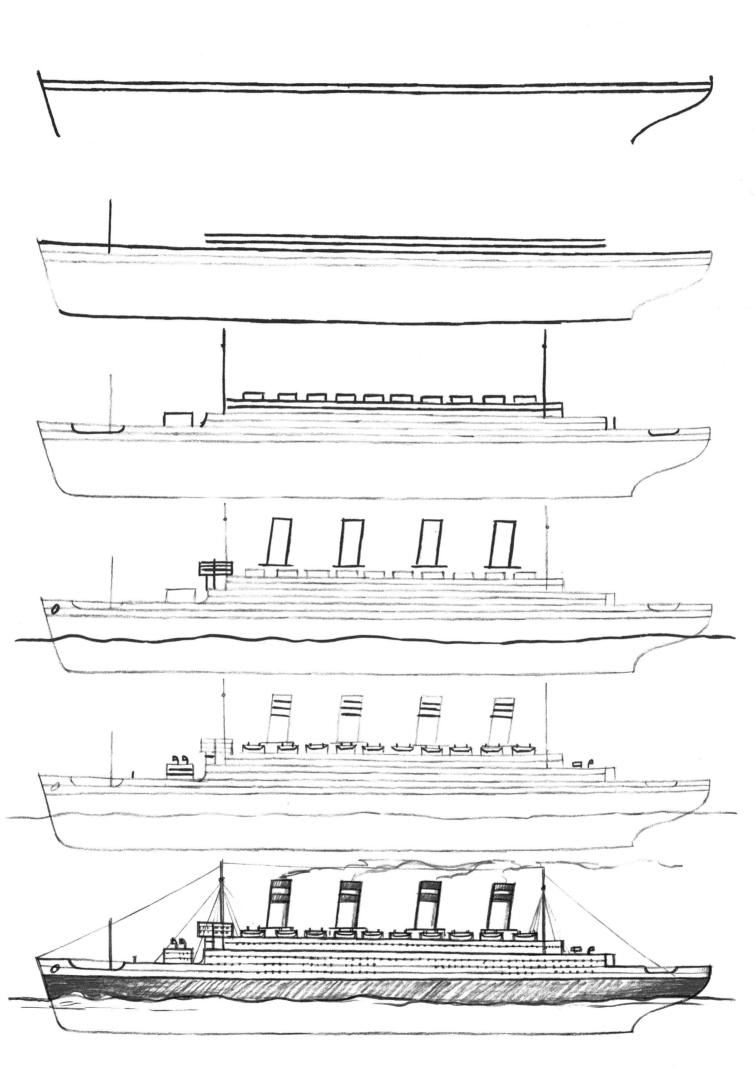

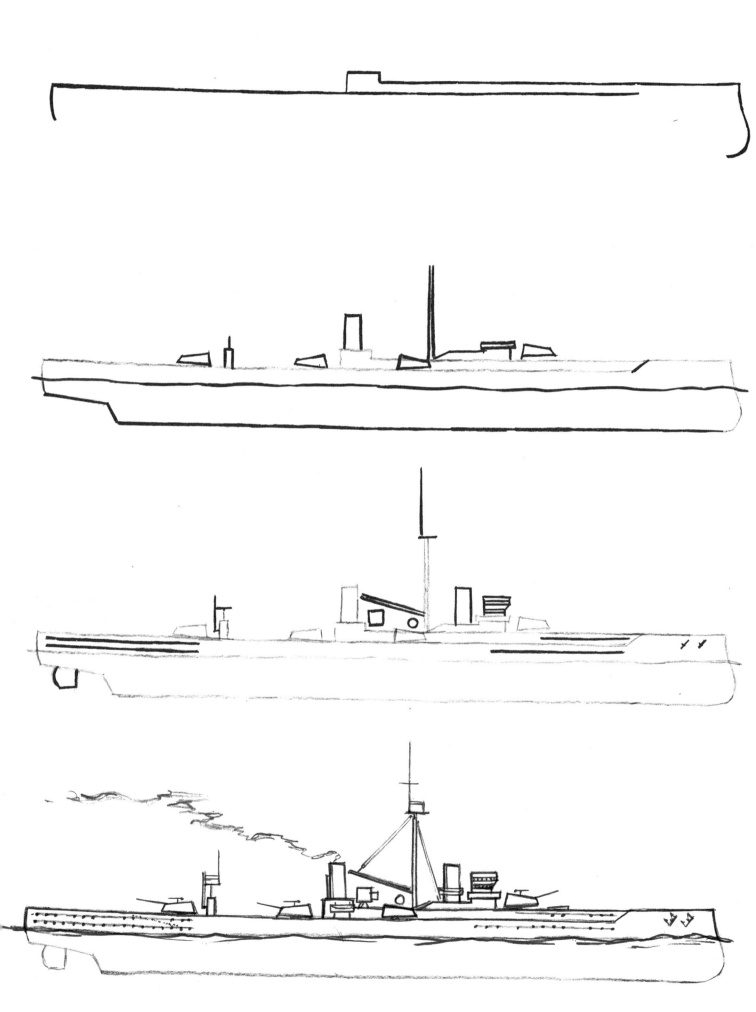

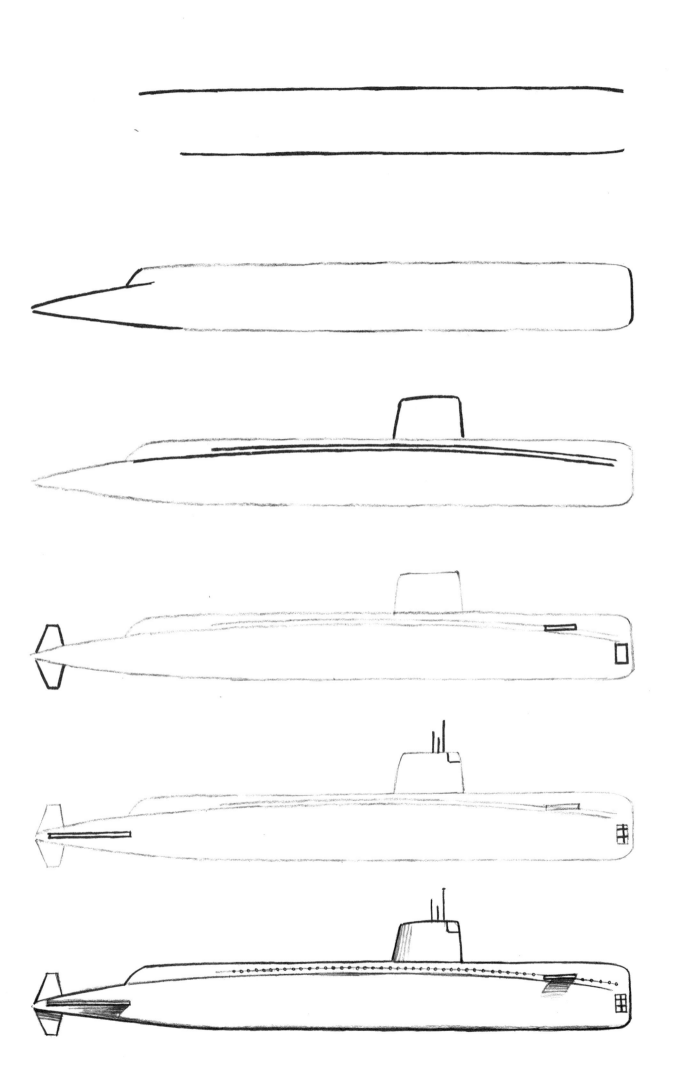

Outrigger

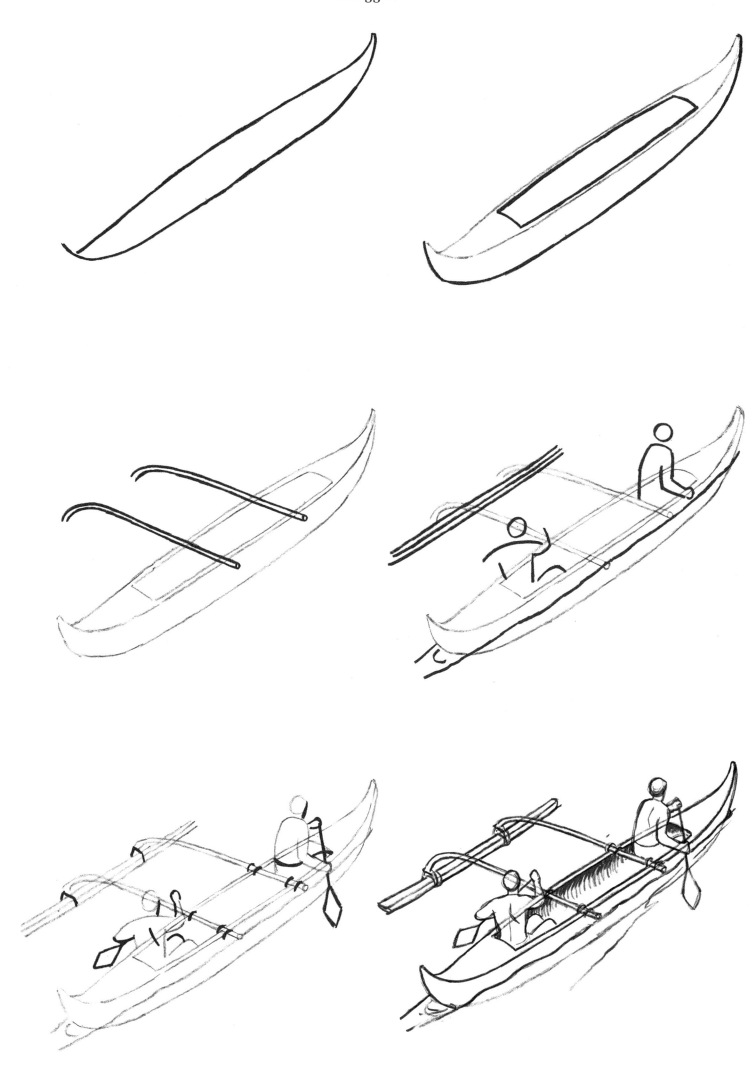

Canoe

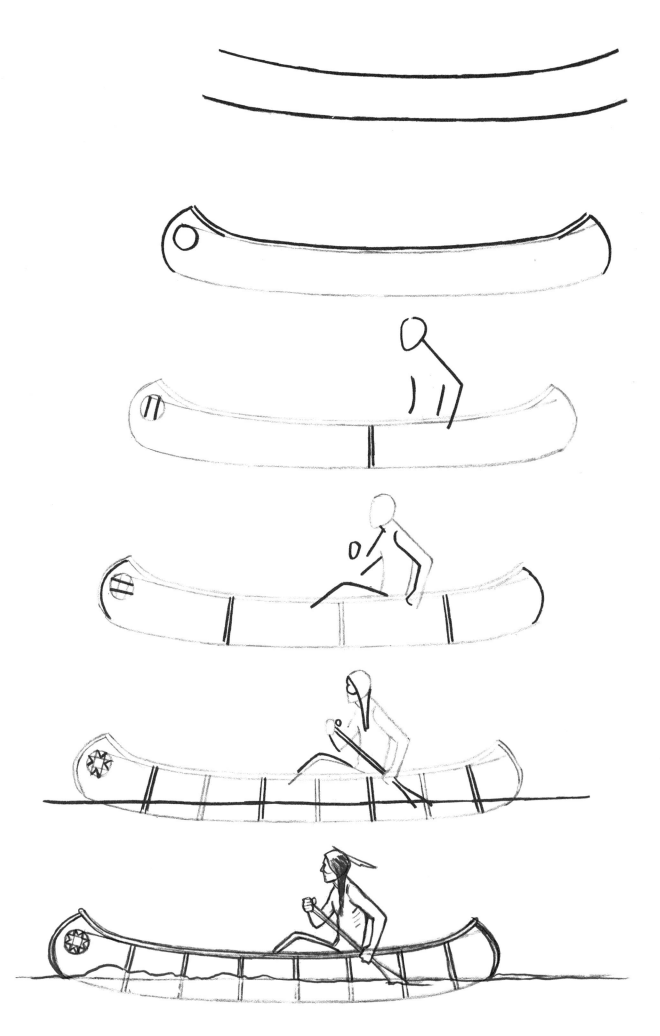

Rowboat

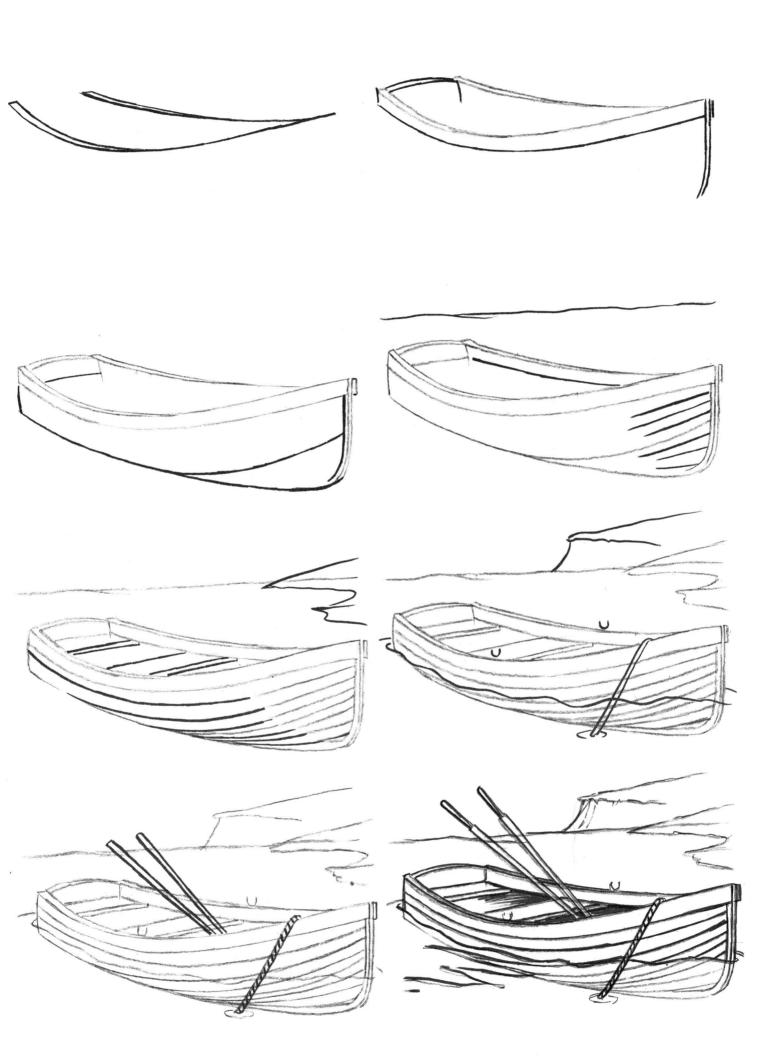

Dory

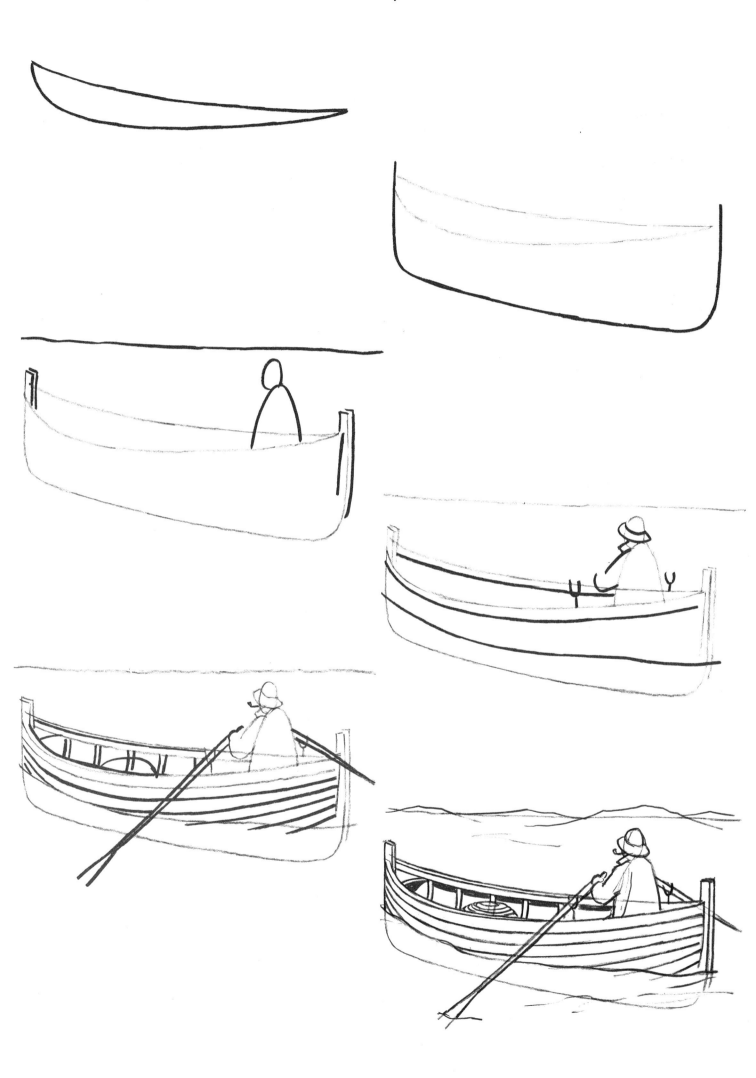

Sampan

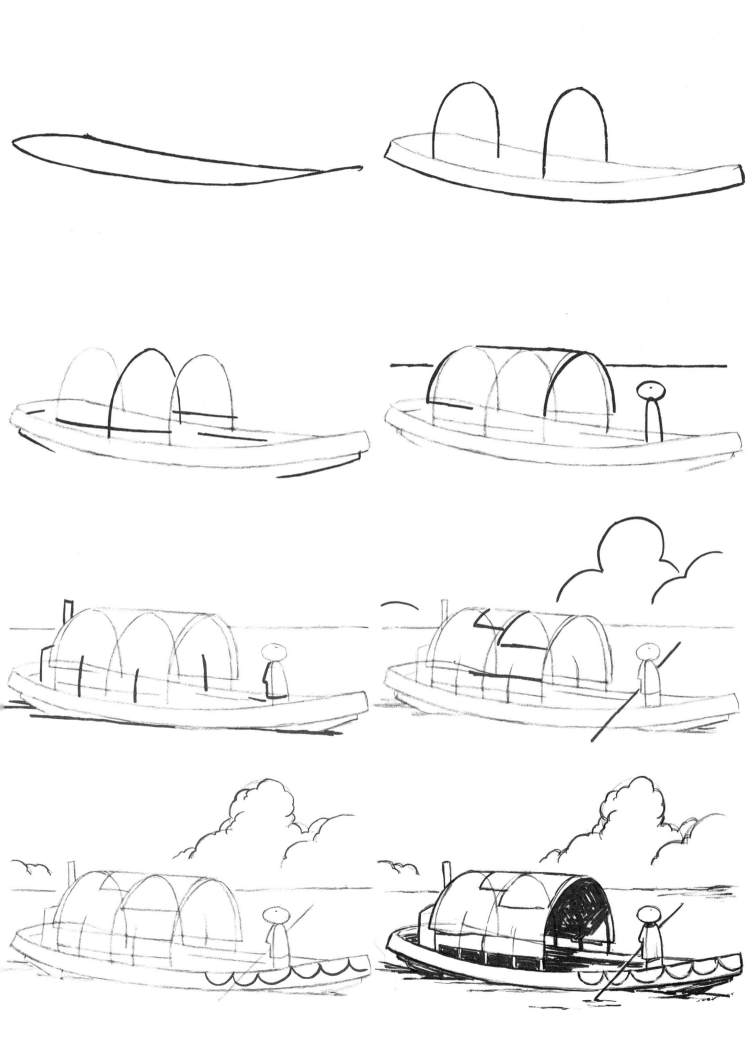

Kayak

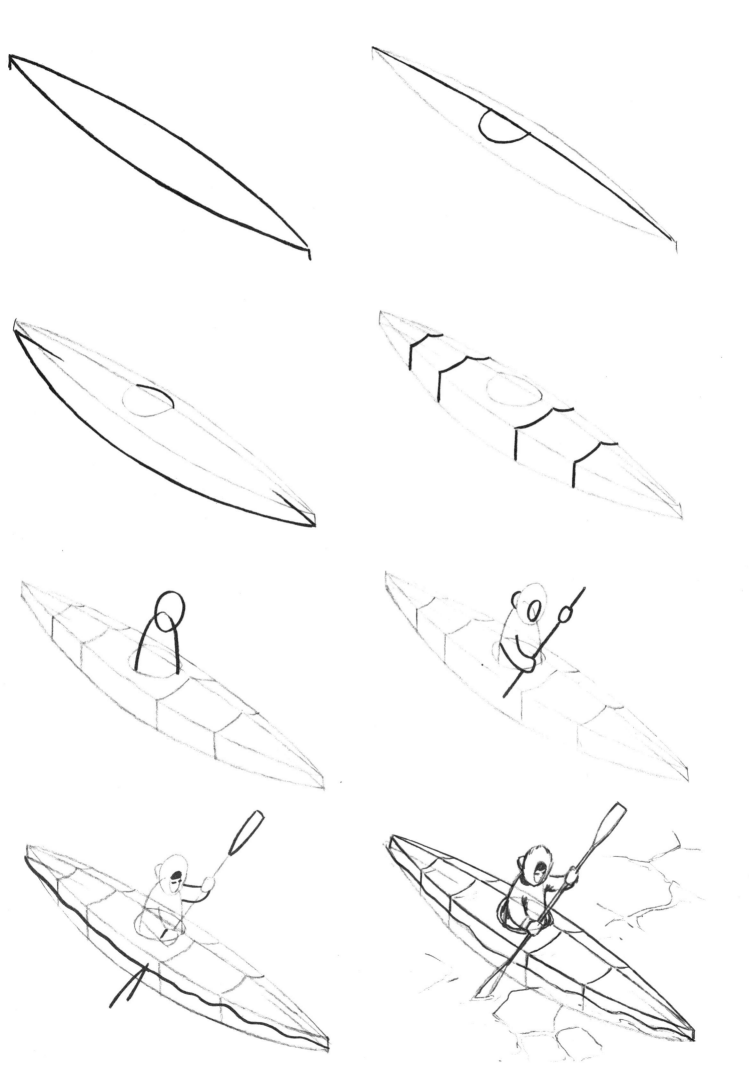

Sloop

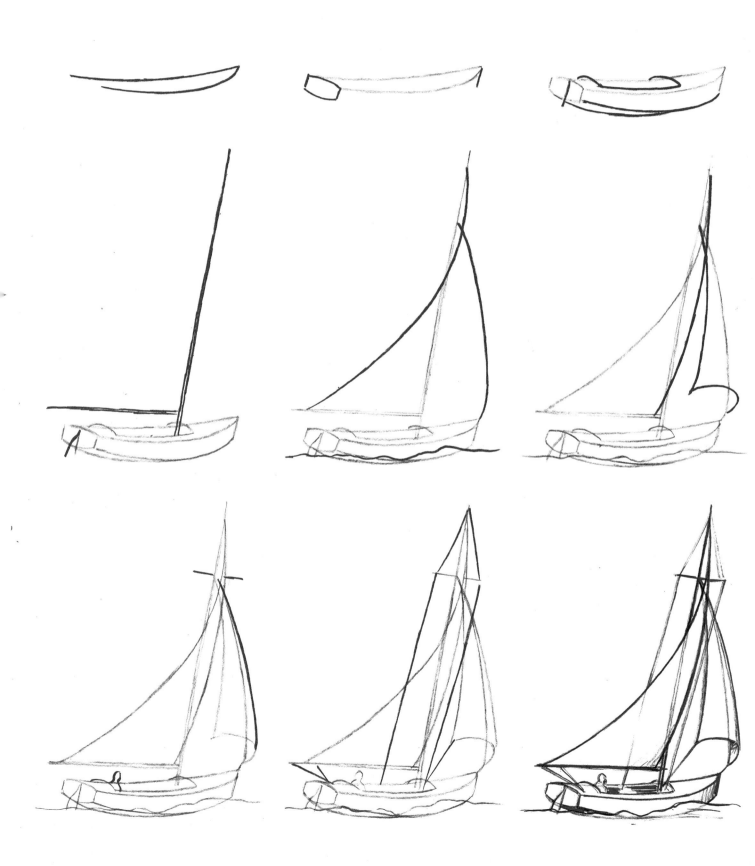

Sloop with Spinnaker

Three-masted Schooner

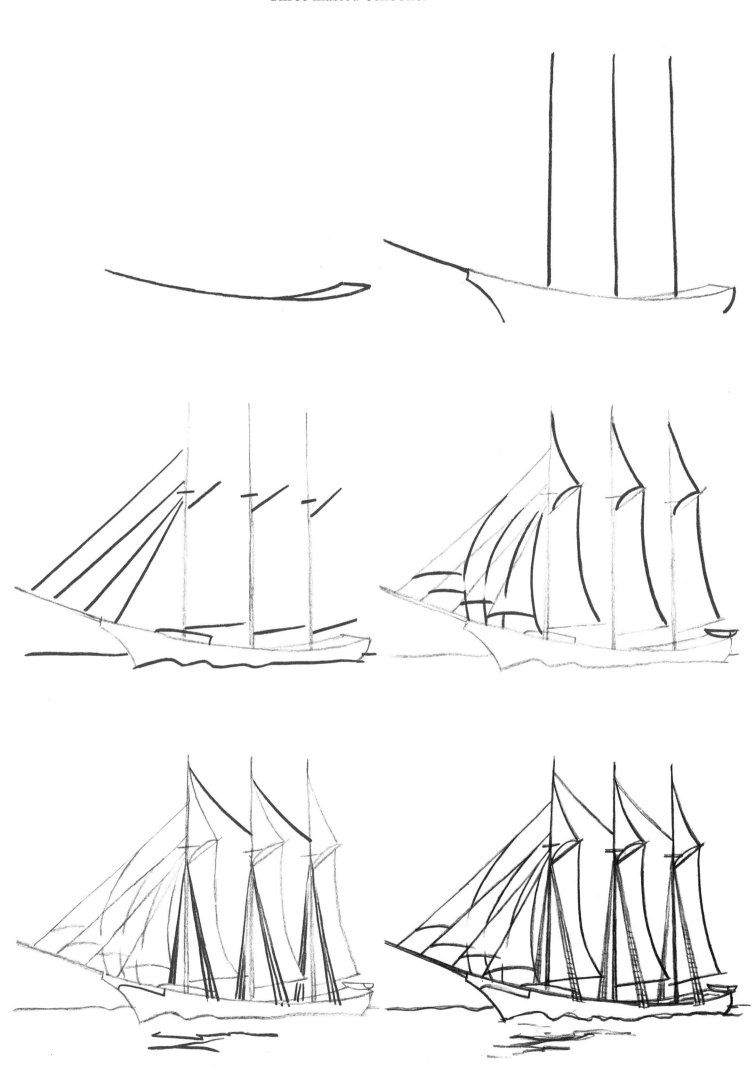

Square-rigged Sailing Ship

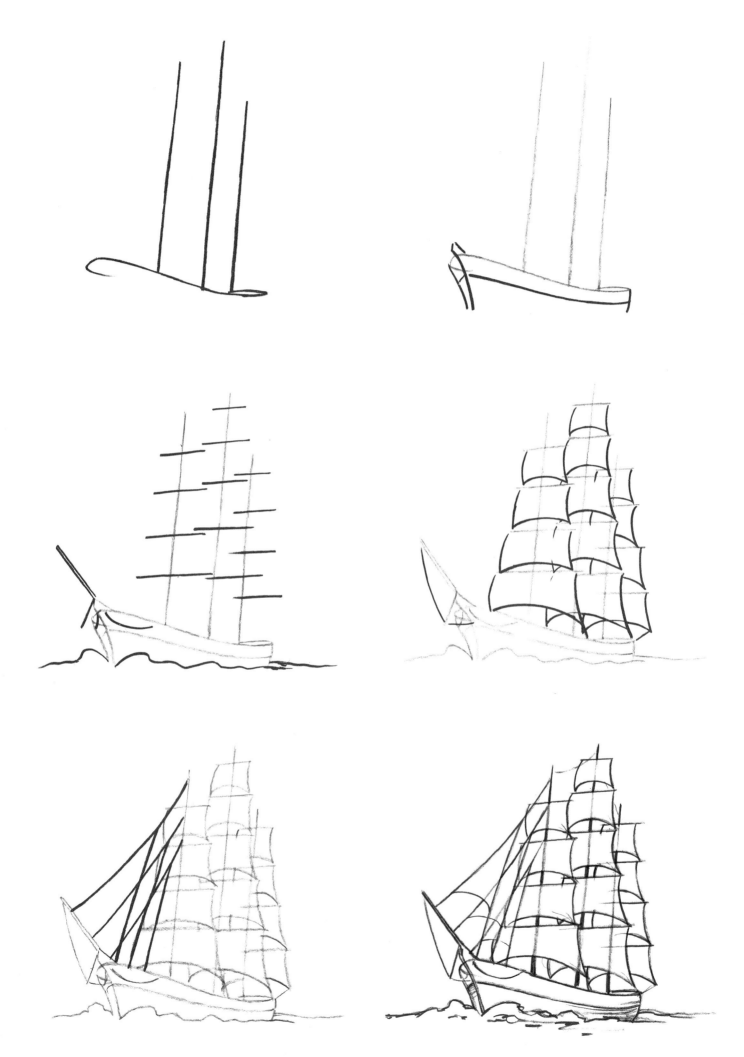

Brigantine

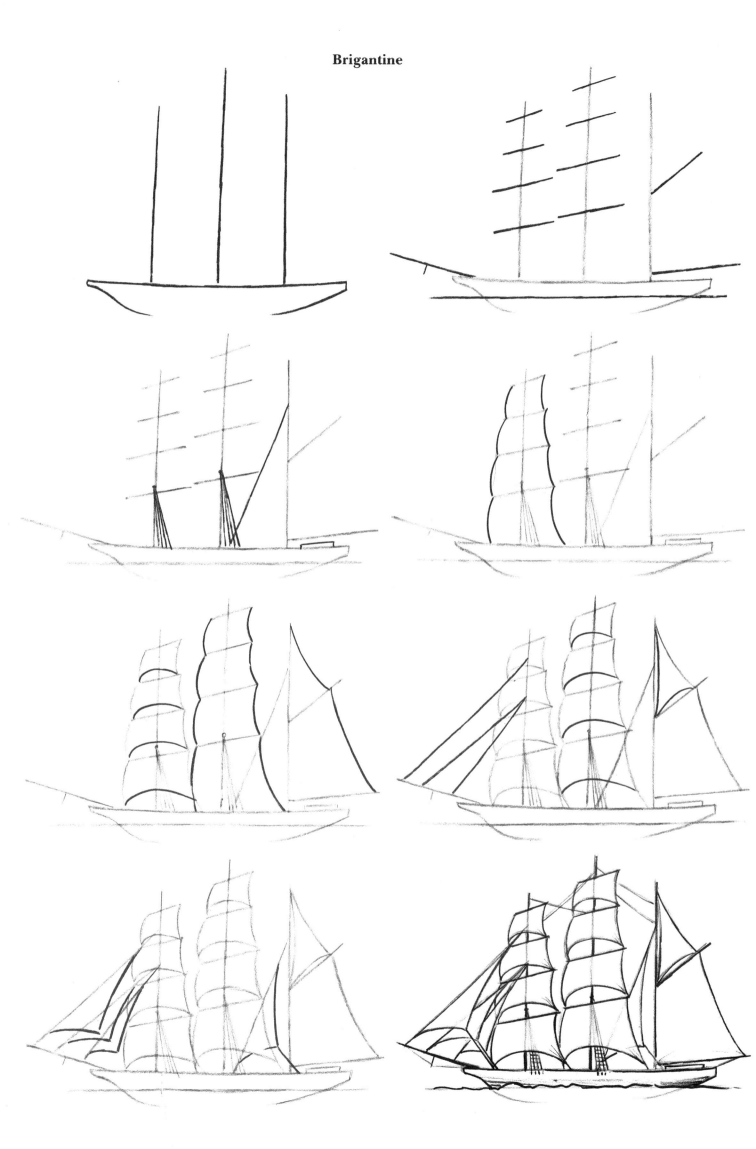

Viking Ship

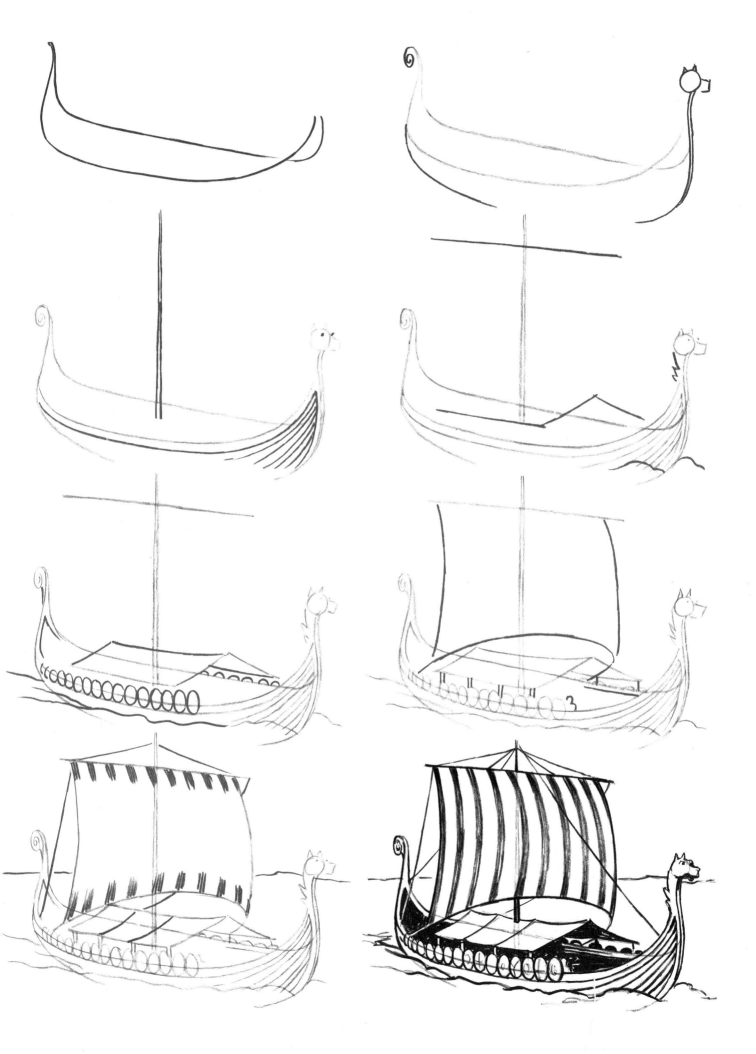

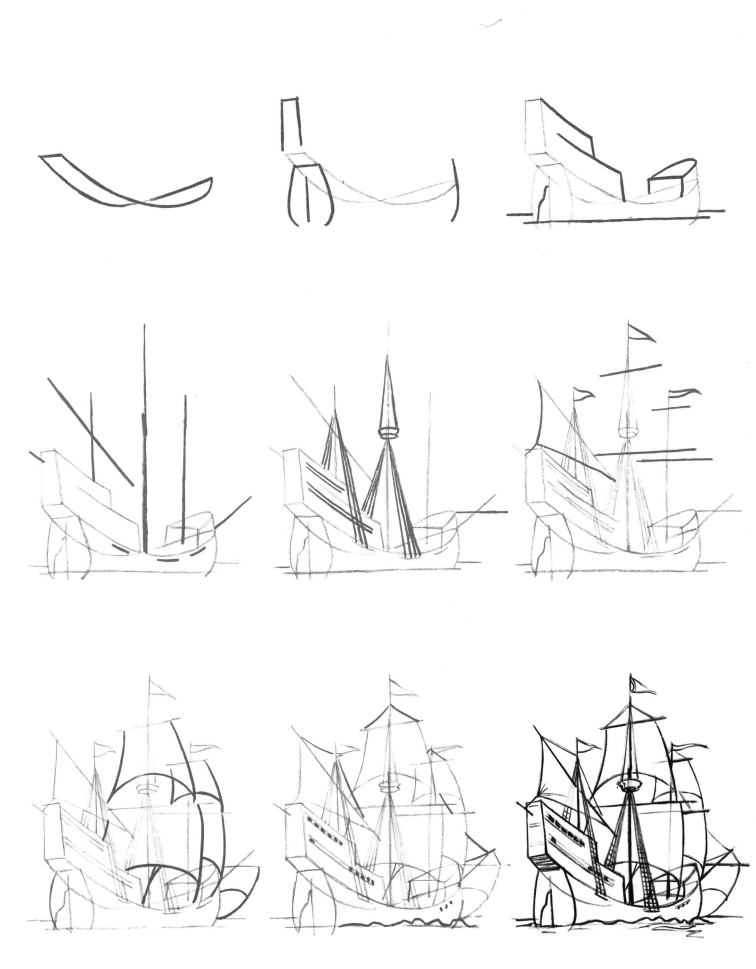

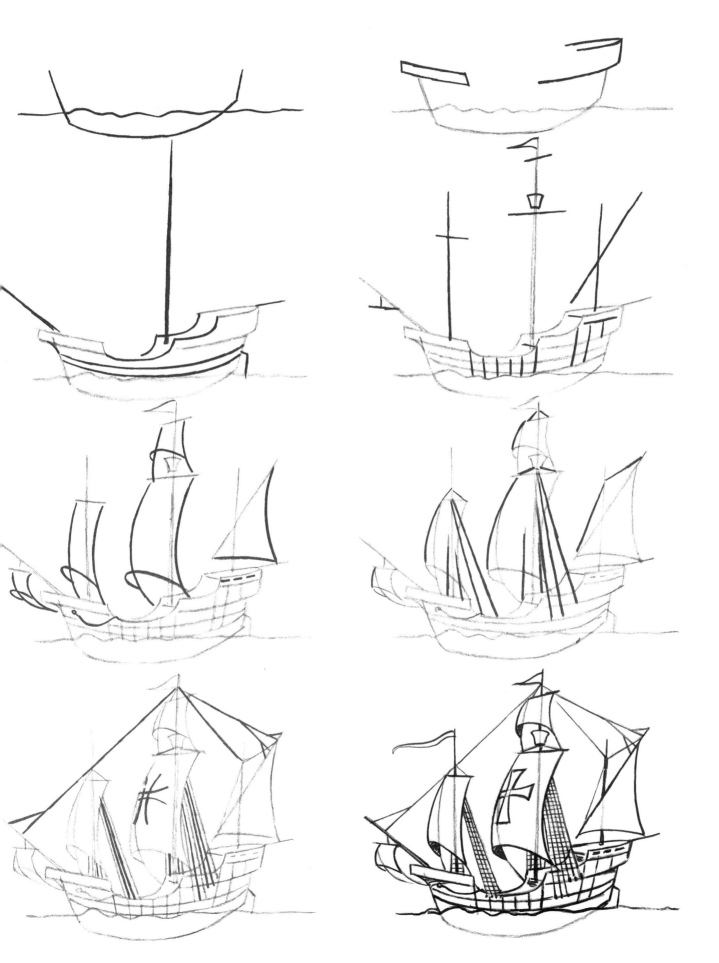

Chinese Junk

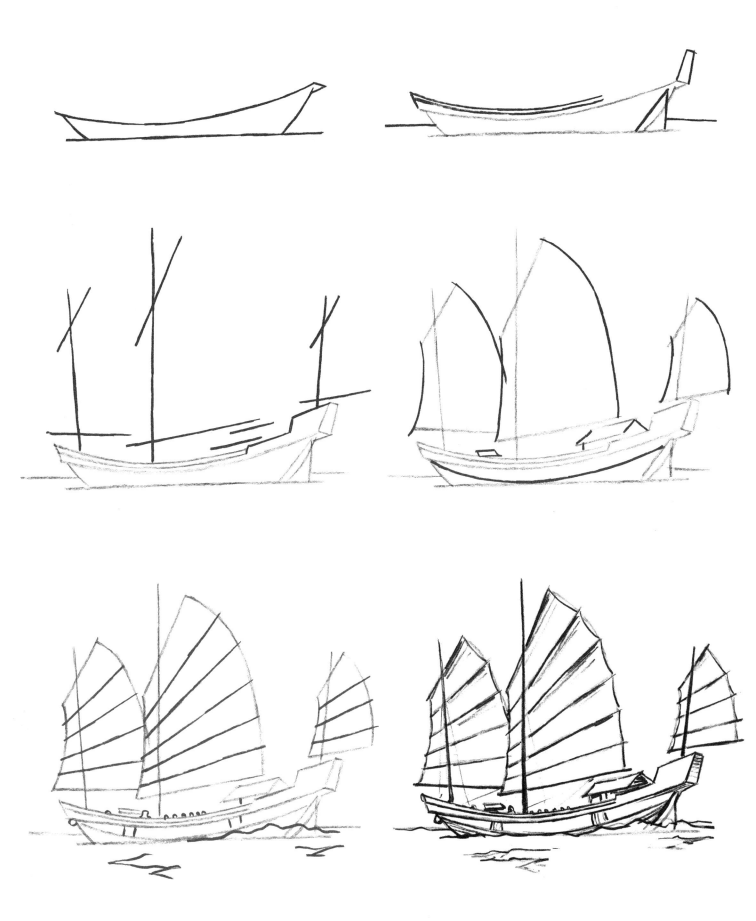

Pickup Truck

Dump Truck

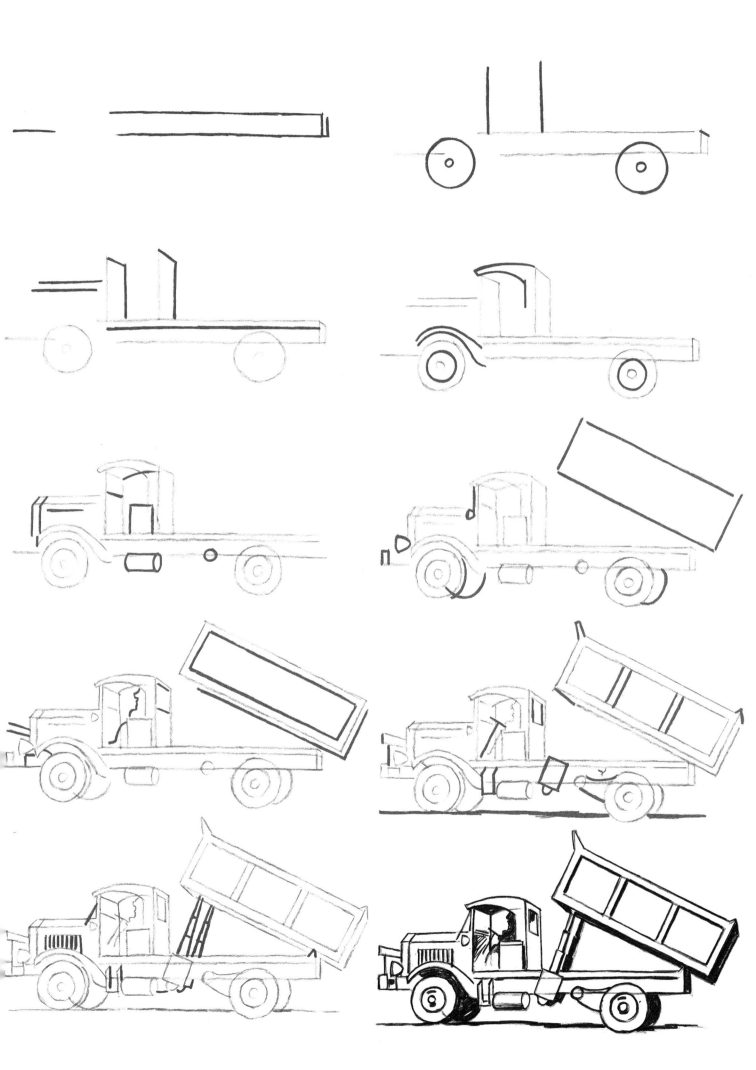

Heavy-duty Truck

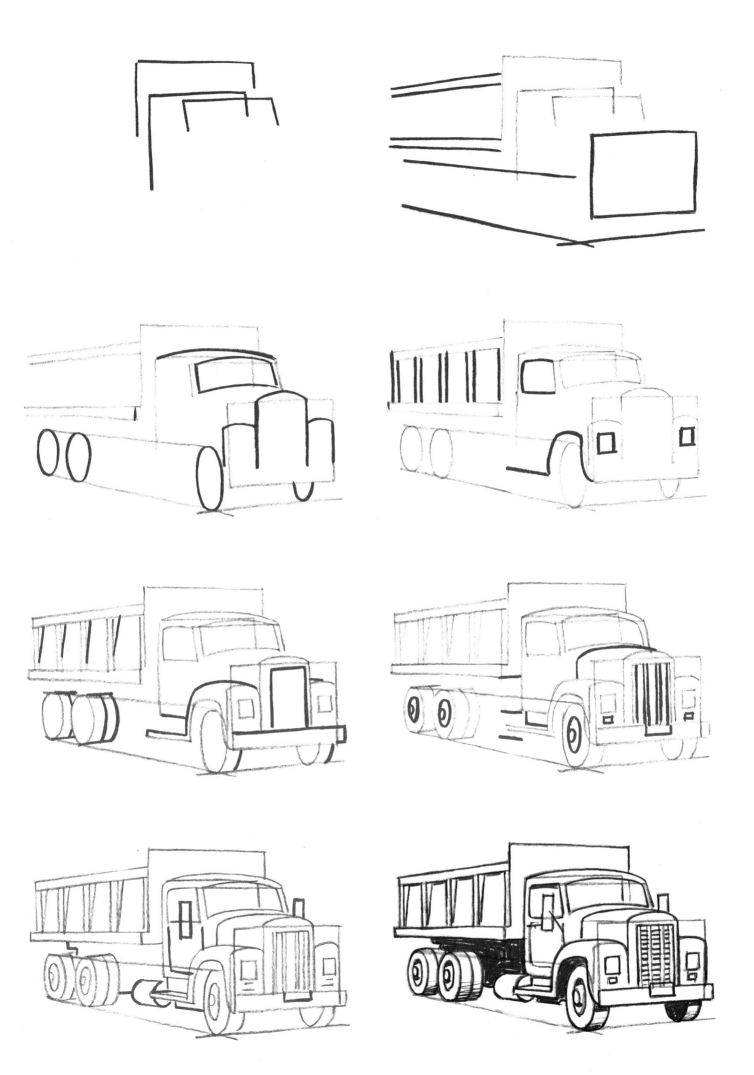

Tractor-trailer

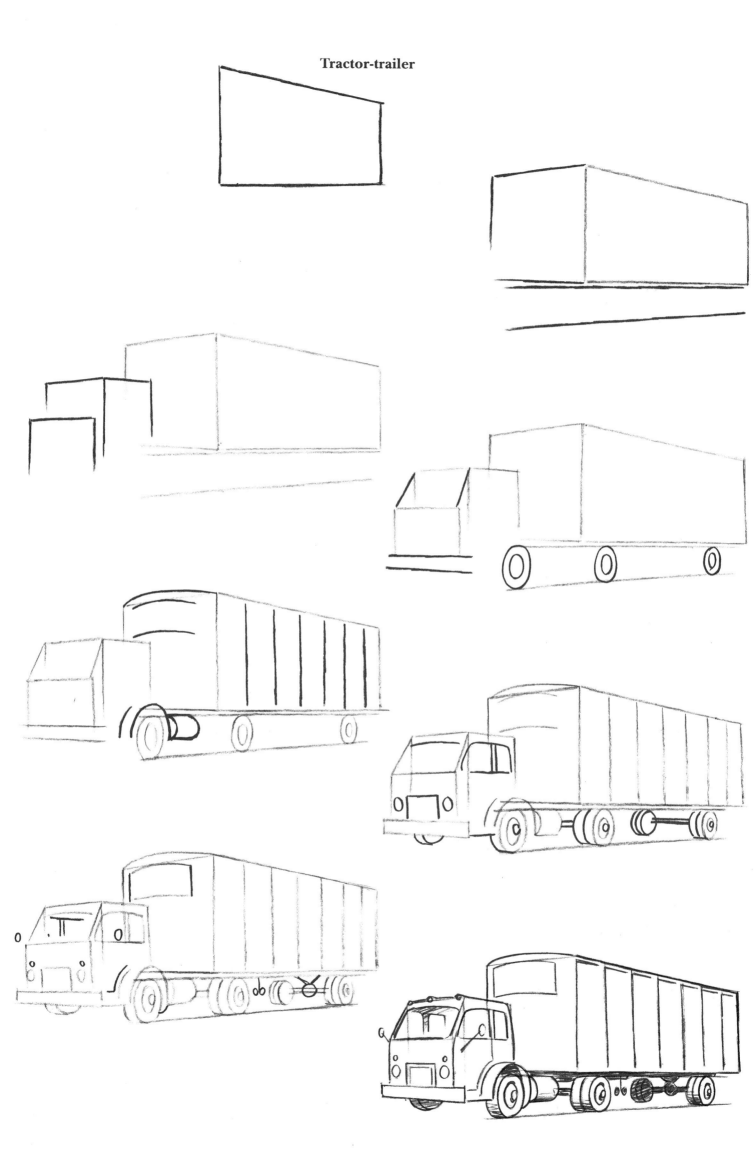

Fire Truck

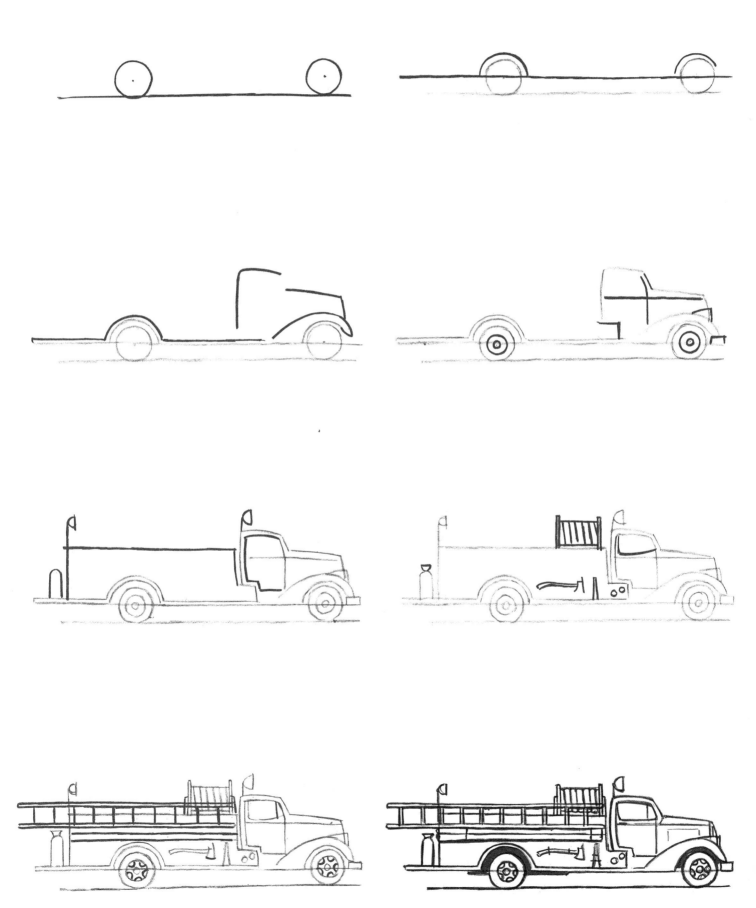

Tanker

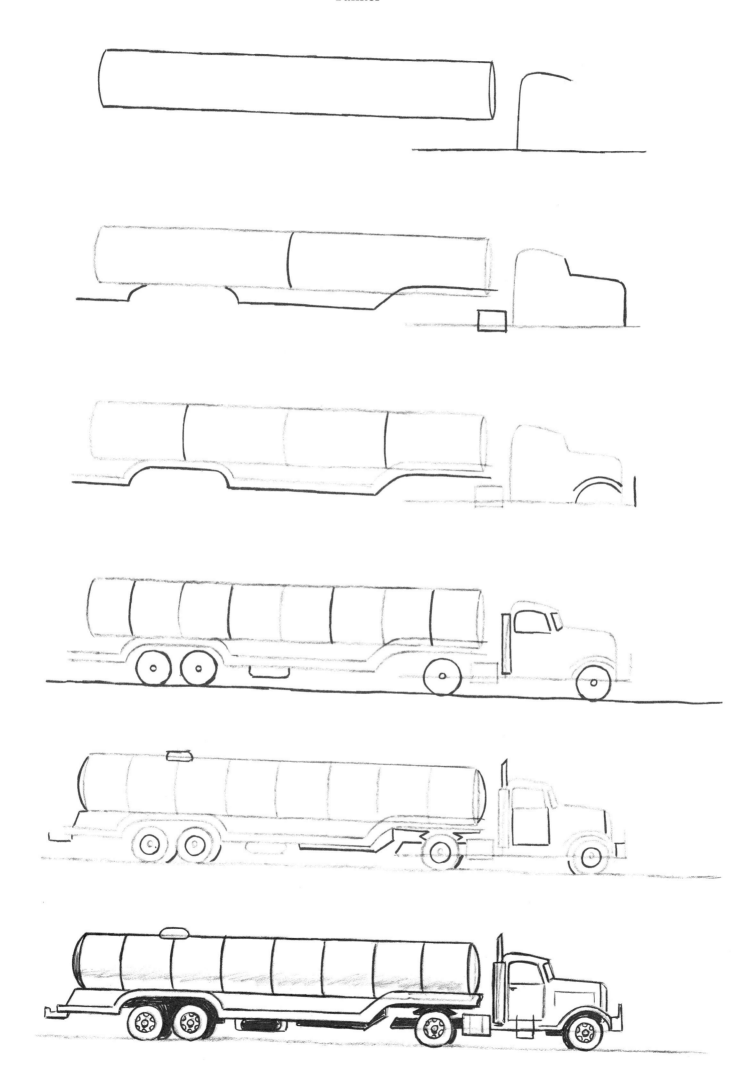

Moving Van

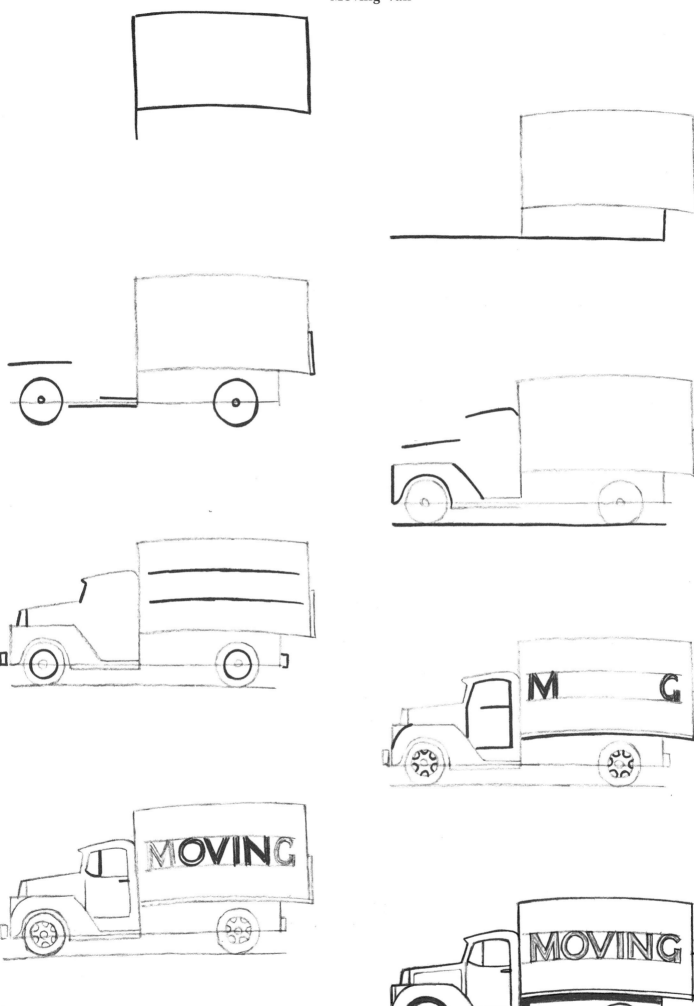

Moving Van

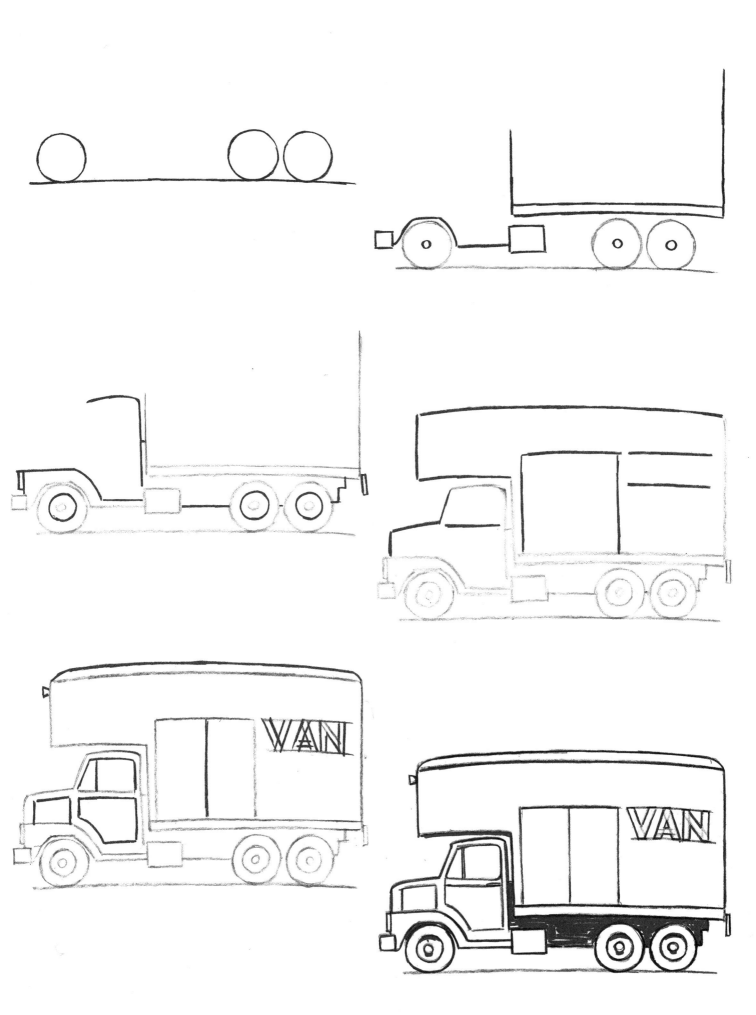

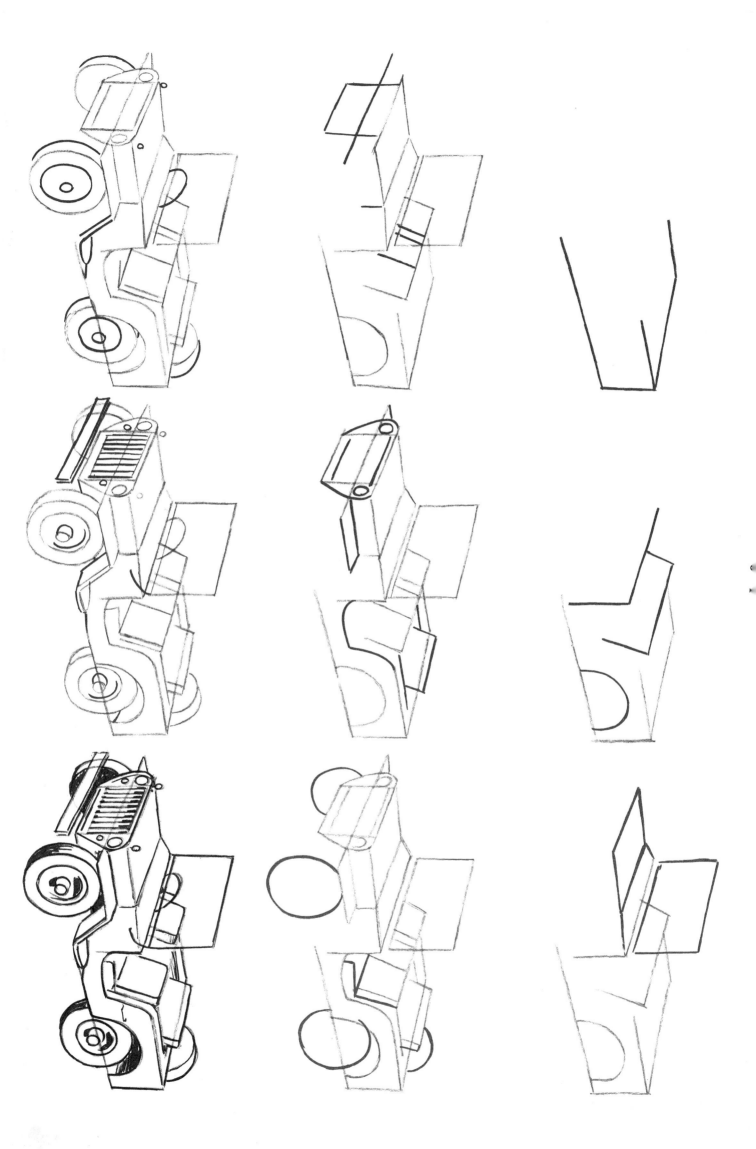

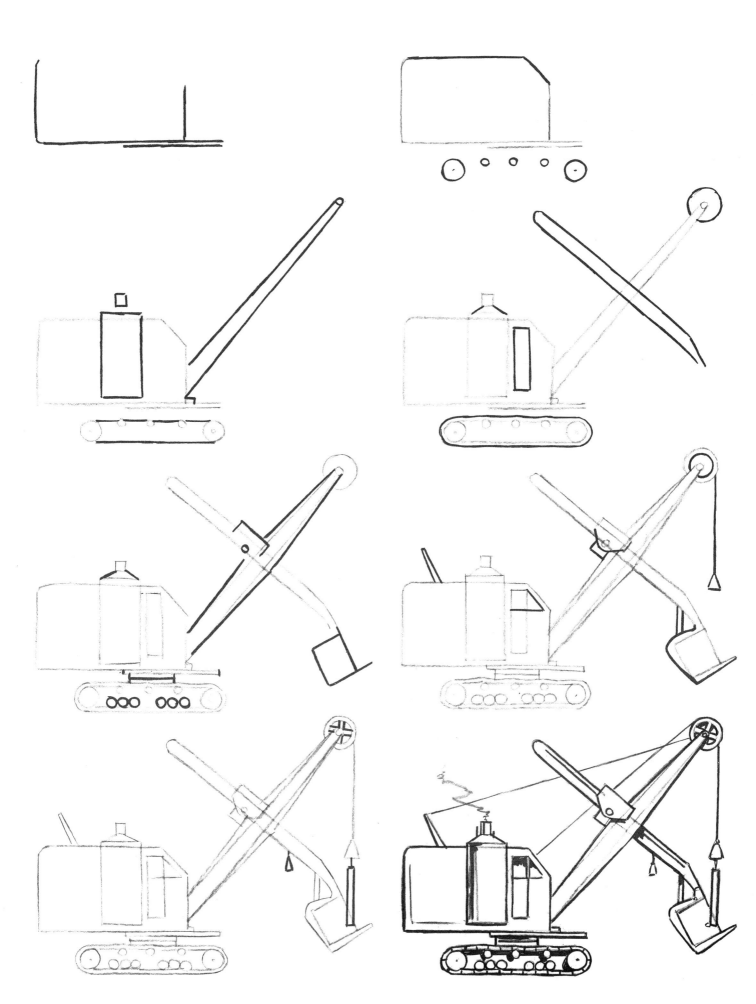

Military Tank

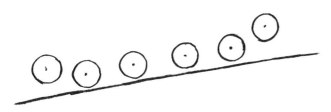
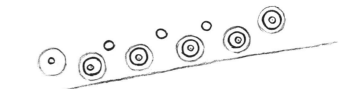
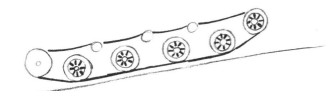
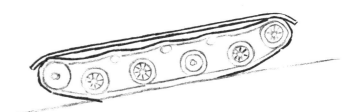
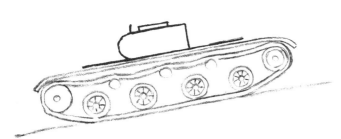
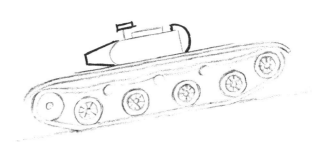
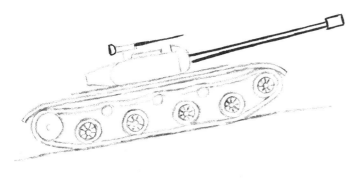
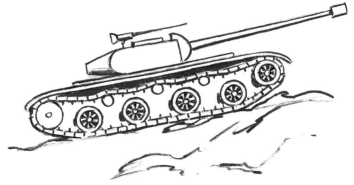

Locomotive (Circa 1865)

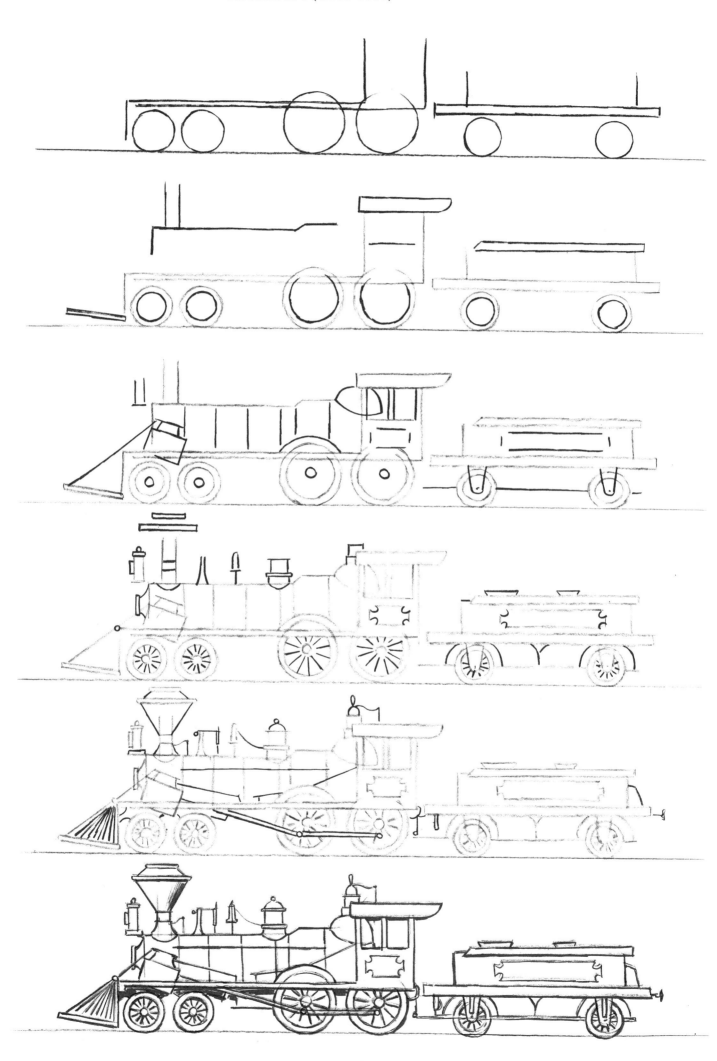

Locomotive (Circa 1879)

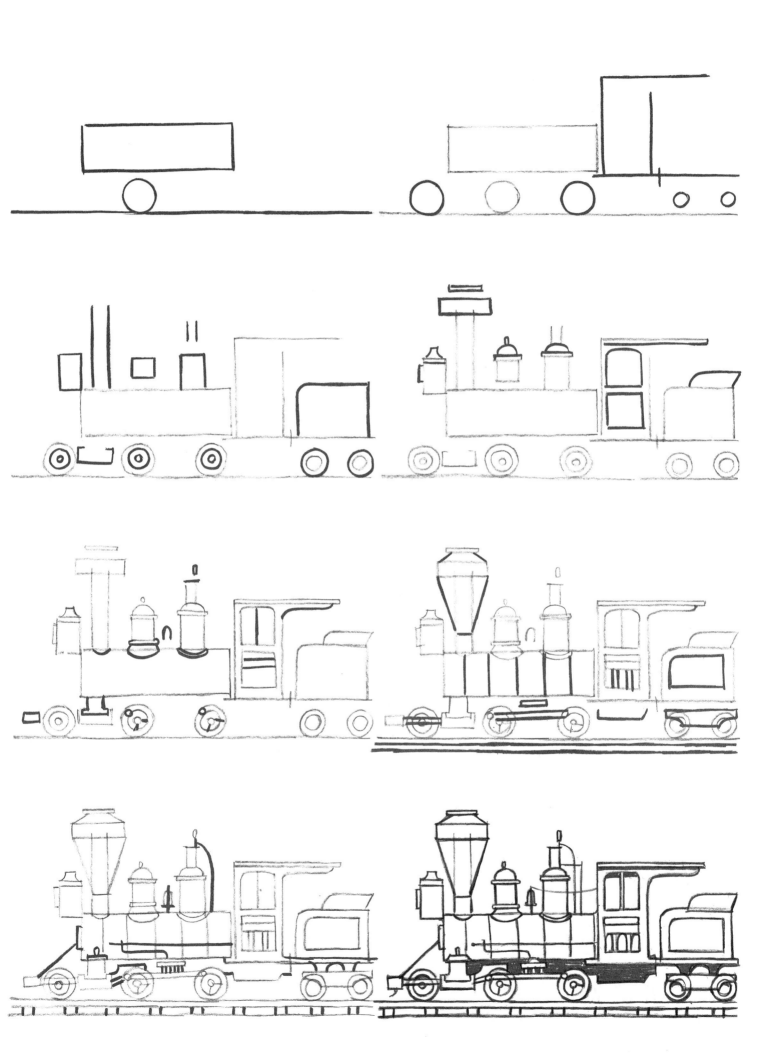

Locomotive (Circa 1893)

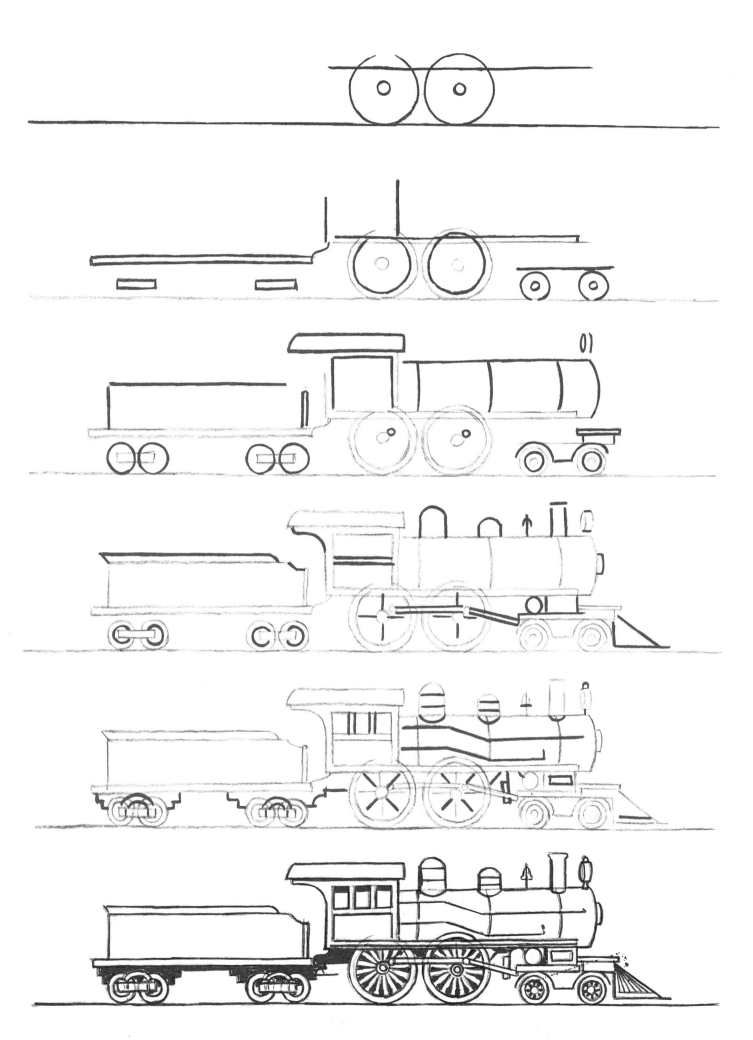

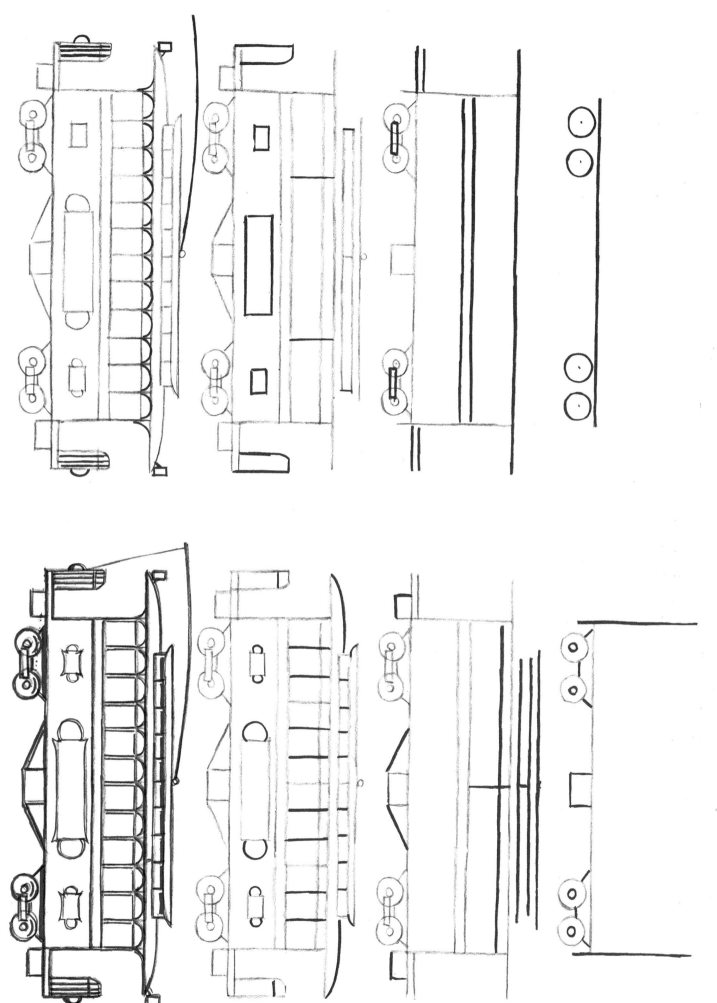

Freight Cars

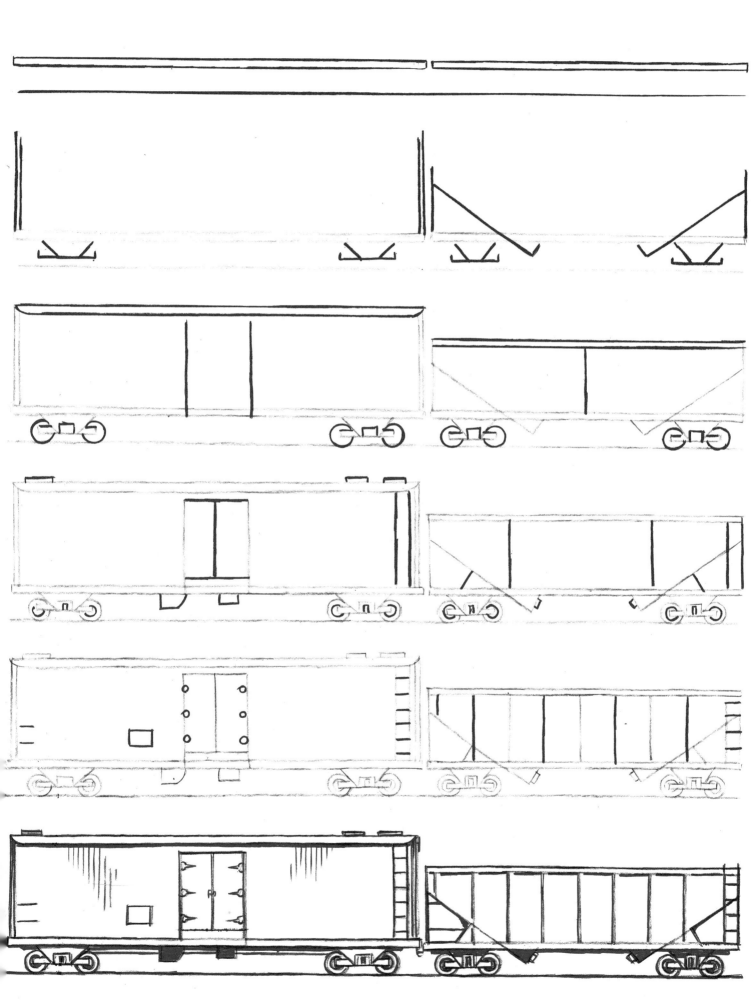

Boxcar and Caboose

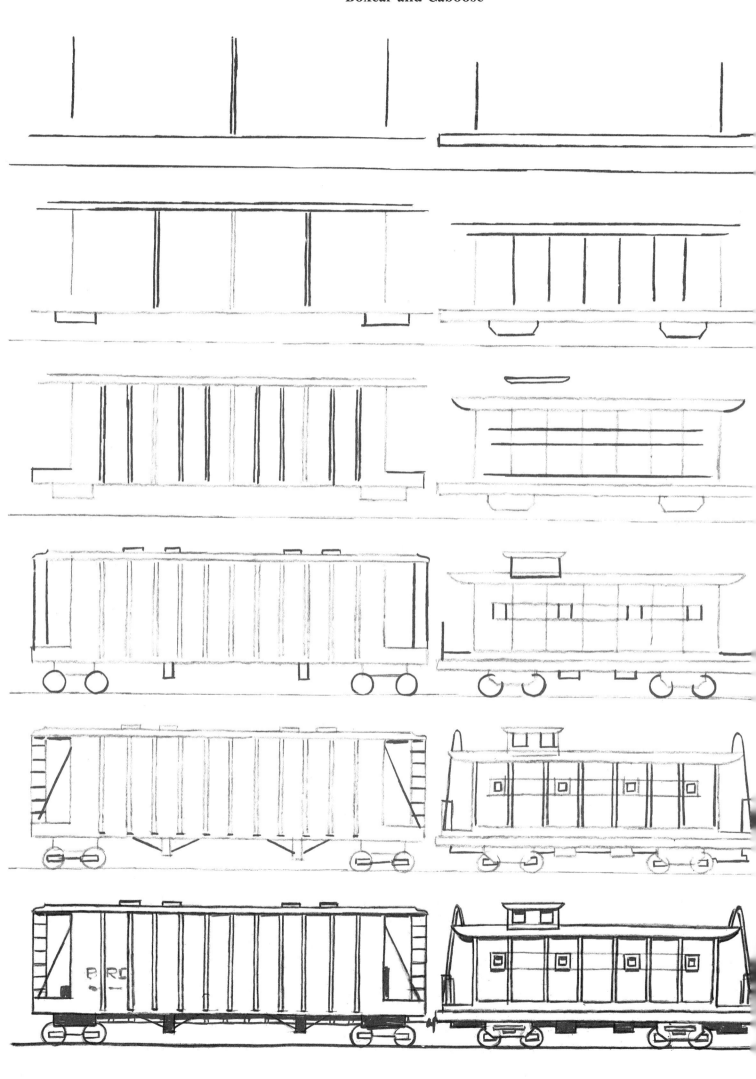

Steam Locomotive

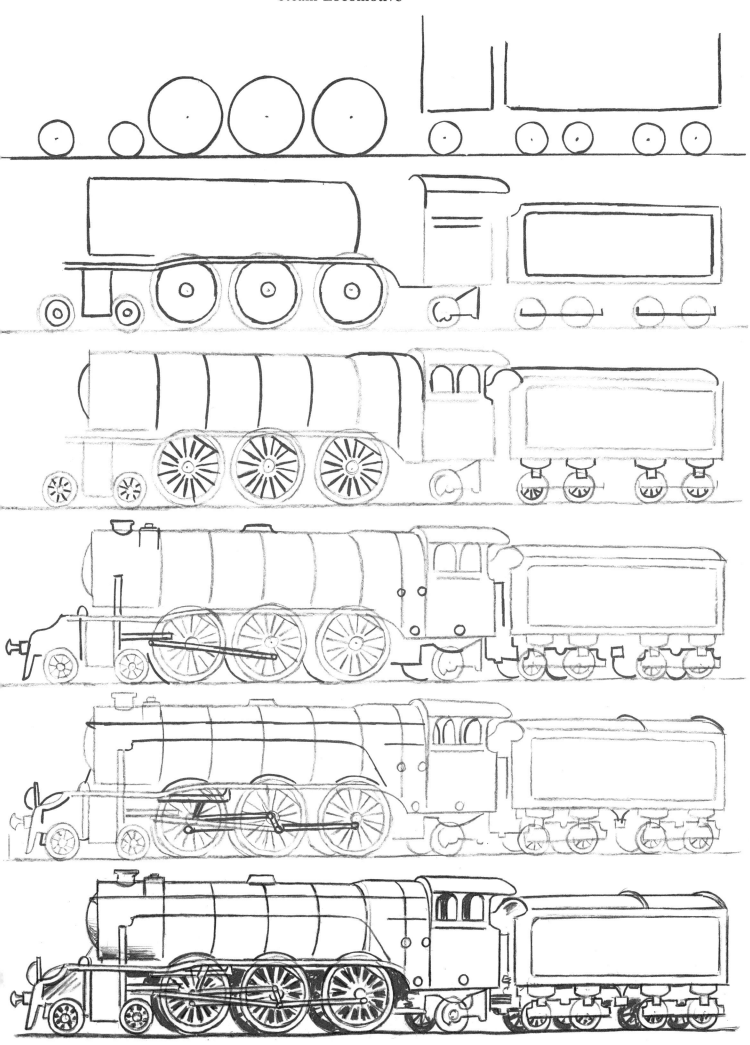

Diesel Streamliner

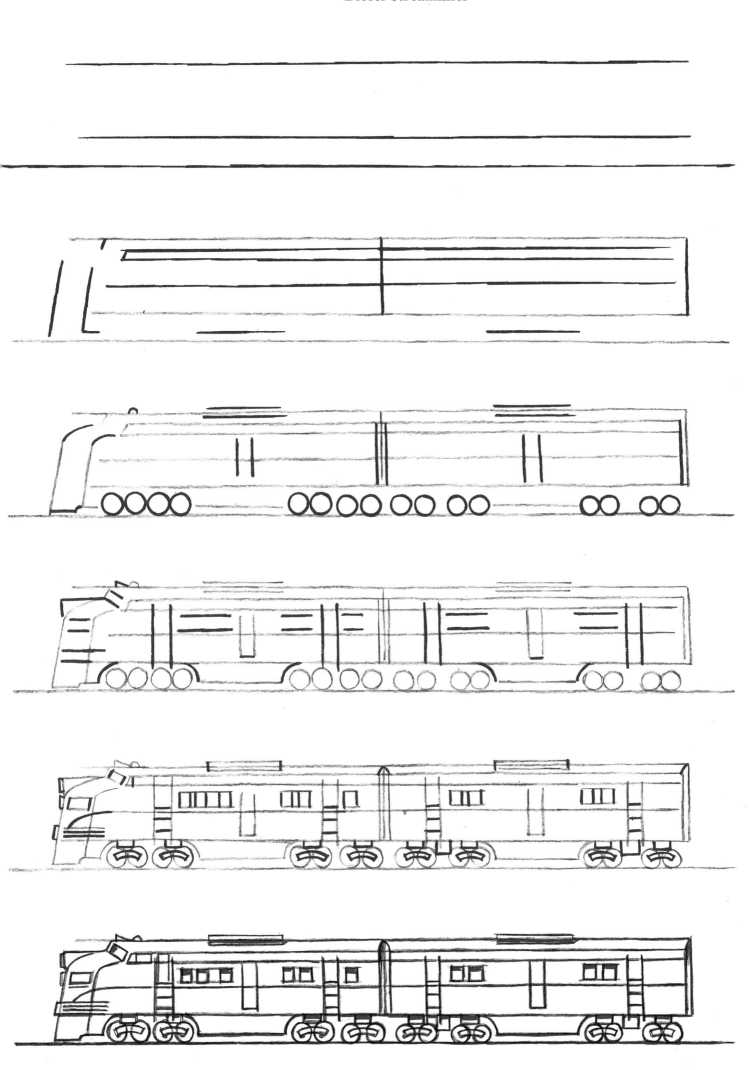

Diesel Streamliner

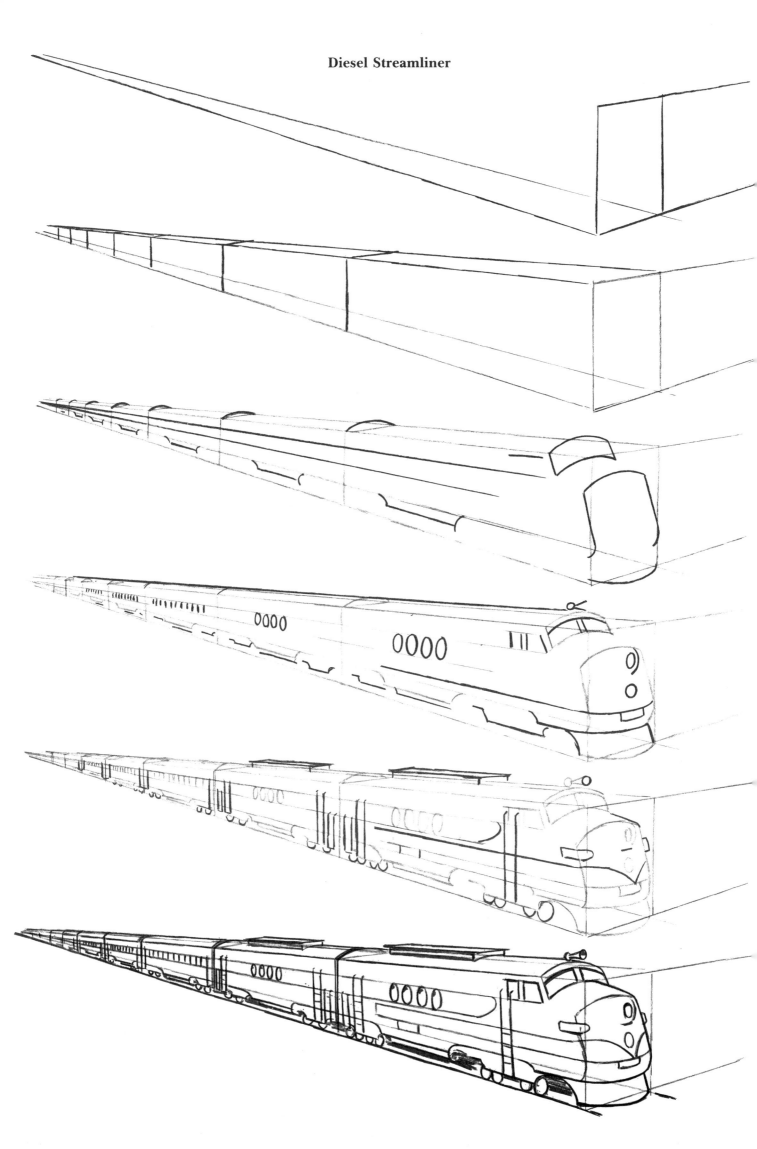

Diesel Streamliner

About the Author

LEE J. AMES joined the Doubleday list in 1962 and has been "drawing 50" ever since. His popular DRAW 50 books have sold over *one million copies* to date!

Lee began his career at Walt Disney Studios and has since taught at the School of Visual Arts in New York City and at Dowling College on Long Island, directed his own advertising agency, and has illustrated over 150 books, from preschool picture books to postgraduate texts.

Lee and his wife Jocelyn live on Long Island, New York.

DRAW 50 FOR HOURS OF FUN!

Using Lee J. Ames's proven, step-by-step method of drawing instruction, you can easily learn to draw animals, monsters, airplanes, cars, sharks, buildings, dinosaurs, famous cartoons, and so much more! Millions of people have learned to draw by using the award-winning "Draw 50" technique. Now you can too!

COLLECT THE ENTIRE DRAW 50 SERIES!

The Draw 50 Series books are available from your local bookstore. You may also order direct (make a copy of this form to order). Titles are paperback, unless otherwise indicated.

ISBN	TITLE	PRICE	QTY	TOTAL
23629-8	Airplanes, Aircraft, and Spacecraft	$8.95/$13.95 Can	× ____	= ____
49145-X	Aliens	$8.95/$13.95 Can	× ____	= ____
19519-2	Animals	$8.95/$13.95 Can	× ____	= ____
90544-X	Animal 'Toons	$8.95/$13.95 Can	× ____	= ____
24638-2	Athletes	$8.95/$13.95 Can	× ____	= ____
26767-3	Beasties and Yugglies and Turnover Uglies and Things That Go Bump in the Night	$8.95/$13.95 Can	× ____	= ____
47163-7	Birds	$8.95/$13.95 Can	× ____	= ____
47006-1	Birds (hardcover)	$13.95/$18.95 Can	× ____	= ____
23630-1	Boats, Ships, Trucks, and Trains	$8.95/$13.95 Can	× ____	= ____
41777-2	Buildings and Other Structures	$8.95/$13.95 Can	× ____	= ____
24639-0	Cars, Trucks, and Motorcycles	$8.95/$13.95 Can	× ____	= ____
24640-4	Cats	$8.95/$13.95 Can	× ____	= ____
42449-3	Creepy Crawlies	$8.95/$13.95 Can	× ____	= ____
19520-6	Dinosaurs and Other Prehistoric Animals	$8.95/$13.95 Can	× ____	= ____
23431-7	Dogs	$8.95/$13.95 Can	× ____	= ____
46985-3	Endangered Animals	$8.95/$13.95 Can	× ____	= ____
19521-4	Famous Cartoons	$8.95/$13.95 Can	× ____	= ____
23432-5	Famous Faces	$8.95/$13.95 Can	× ____	= ____
47150-5	Flowers, Trees, and Other Plants	$8.95/$13.95 Can	× ____	= ____
26770-3	Holiday Decorations	$8.95/$13.95 Can	× ____	= ____
17642-2	Horses	$8.95/$13.95 Can	× ____	= ____
17639-2	Monsters	$8.95/$13.95 Can	× ____	= ____
41194-4	People	$8.95/$13.95 Can	× ____	= ____
47162-9	People of the Bible	$8.95/$13.95 Can	× ____	= ____
47005-3	People of the Bible (hardcover)	$13.95/$19.95 Can	× ____	= ____
26768-1	Sharks, Whales, and Other Sea Creatures	$8.95/$13.95 Can	× ____	= ____
14154-8	Vehicles	$8.95/$13.95 Can	× ____	= ____
	Shipping and handling	(add $2.50 per order)× ____		= ____
		TOTAL		____

Please send me the title(s) I have indicated above. I am enclosing $_____.

Send check or money order in U.S. funds only (no C.O.D.s or cash, please). Make check payable to Random House, Inc. Allow 4–6 weeks for delivery. Prices and availability subject to change without notice.

Name: _____

Address: _____ Apt. #_____

City: _____ State: _____ Zip: _____

Send completed coupon and payment to:

Random House, Inc.
Customer Service
400 Hahn Rd.
Westminster, MD 21157

BROADWAY